THE WAITING ROOM

A POCKET-SIZE MANUSCRIPT
ABOUT LIFE AND LIVING

Angela Marie Zimmerman
and Dorothy Teresia Zimmerman

Editor
Mary T. Abbruscato

ISBN 979-8-88540-637-6 (paperback)
ISBN 979-8-88540-638-3 (digital)

Christian Faith Publishing, Inc.
832 Park Avenue
Meadville, PA 16335
www.christianfaithpublishing.com

Printed in the United States of America

To Paul, whose life lessons and spirit have fueled our
hearts and will remain a presence in our lives forever.

Contents

Preface

Throughout our lives, we all need a place to be, to contribute, to belong, and to be loved. These elements define us and help create *our story*. At times, the dynamic nature of life can take us to places that extend us well beyond our means and make us feel as if we have no control over our destiny. When we enter these places, these life moments *in the waiting room,* there *are* options to embrace. If we allow our eyes to see and our hearts to behold, we can readily integrate these lessons learned. Because it is truly in *living* in this w*aiting room* that we can return to the next challenge with renewed strength and insight *and* greet our next triumph with a lens that acknowledges and celebrates the attainment of these gifts that further our human development and connection. The greatest present we can give each other (and ourselves) is this time, and yet one of our greatest fears is that of authentically being connected.

These are among the many prolific revelations reflected upon as we frequent the timeless *waiting room.*

Acknowledgement

Our family is indebted to Deborah Barrett-Anderson who listened intently to these stories and inspired us to chronicle this journey. Capturing and recording these experiences, in and of itself, has deeply enriched our lives, and we humbly thank you!

The Life and Times

There's no vocabulary for love within a family,
love that's lived in but not looked at, love within
the light of which all else is seen, the love within
which all other love finds speech. This love is
silent.

—T.S. Eliot

The waiting room can be a place in your mind, anticipating life events, challenges, and opportunities; or a physical location, an environment where you wait in anticipation of the outcome of others. One of the most important life lessons learned in the waiting room is that of redirecting your energy away from things over which you have minimal control. Everyone enters the waiting room at very deliberate times in their life—at times for reasons unknown—but everyone passes through. What you do with these lessons learned can transform your life forever. Here is one life's passage in that place, a journey of an ordinary family through extraordinary experiences in the waiting room.

These are reflections about a man, his family, and the impact, not the end but the beginning of reflection, healing, reconciliation, and, hopefully, peace.

And so, it began.

In 1935, Paul was born to Angelina, an Italian immigrant, three times married. This, her third marriage, was quite unexpected and surprisingly embraced. For Angelina, marriages did not endure, happiness was not in the forecast, and her children were her legacy, her only hope to make a difference and contribution to the world.

Angelina was a single mother of four and widowed twice after her first husband became a victim of a homemade bomb explosion and the second died in a motorcycle accident. She had an indomitable spirit, was creative, and possessive of her greatest assets, her children. Her resilience was only exceeded by her pride in them. For her, the sun rose and set upon them and provided purpose in her life and survival.

Thinking life would never include a true soul mate and that dependence was on herself, she persevered the best way she knew how. As a seamstress, Angelina made a modest living and was a day-to-day survivor. Her son Anthony was the youngest of four—two boys and two girls. The family relied on his charisma and communication skills to navigate the social network of their small neighborhood. Having the personality he was known for, Anthony cheerfully welcomed a new neighbor, Mr. Zimmerman, to the community by his warm smile and curious introductions. Mr. Z, as this older German fellow was later affectionately named, was a quiet, reserved man who stayed to himself. He was a paint dyer who retired from his service as a fireman on foreign ships, had no family in America, and had limited friends and interaction in the neighborhood.

At the time of this fateful meeting, young Anthony's mind was preoccupied with the usual concerns of his family's survival; that is, food, rent, and many other realities that should never have troubled those of a child his age. Mr. Z, being the intuitive man he was, immediately sensed the worries of this young lad and prompted Anthony to confide in him. Into the ears of this kind stranger, Anthony told of his struggling family's circumstances. Upon hearing the troubling hardships suffered by this loving family, Mr. Z gave Anthony a comforting hug, assuring him that this was not something a young boy should be worried about. He reinforced that everything would work out in its intended time. He then bid goodbye to his new little friend, taking with him all the worries from Anthony's tender, young shoulders.

With the dawn of the next day came the beginning of a new life for little Anthony and the answer to his family's undying prayers. Angelina awoke to find a basket of food at her doorstep for her hungry children and a bucket of coal to keep them warm. Not knowing where these life-saving gifts came from, Angelina tempered her pride to accept them. Her family's need to survive outweighed her strong feelings of independence. She would soon come to realize that an unexpected *earth angel* was in the midst, and life would no longer be the same. As the days passed and gifts continued to be left, ongoing thoughts continued to race in her mind, questioning, What if this is a mistake? Why is someone helping us? What is their intention? These troubling concerns continued with each new delivery.

Unaware of these acts of kindness, little Anthony's friendship with Mr. Z flourished, and life became happier in his family home. With a newfound hope and great excitement, Anthony began telling his mother tales of his new acquaintance and how it was Mr. Z who predicted that his family's struggles would be resolved. In his little heart, he knew that Mr. Z was right, for things were looking better! Angelina enjoyed her son's excitement and enthusiasm as he shared his accounts of this fateful yet unusual union, not fully understanding the true depth of their friendship. Nonetheless, she was truly inspired by the messages of hope her beautiful young son displayed to her during these heartfelt conversations.

As the weeks went by and the doorstep deliveries continued to arrive, Angelina's increasing curiosity also continued, drowning out her need to just accept them without question. Arising with the break of a new day, Angelina sat by her window hoping to discover the identity of her family's sponsor. As if right on cue, Mr. Z arrived bearing the usual gifts, quietly attempting to leave them without notice. Although reticent at first, Angelina opened the door and hesitantly introduced herself. Noticing that the deliverer was an older gentleman, she questioned his intentions and told him that his "gifts" were no longer welcome. With the economy diminished and her financial means limited, she displayed her prideful spirit, insisting that she would only accept these items in exchange for her services of cooking, cleaning, and/or sewing. She declared that she would not accept charity from anyone, especially a total stranger. Realizing Angelina's need for independence, Mr. Z agreed to her terms and allowed her to maintain the pride she held close to her being. As time went on, and as fate would have it, Angelina became reliant on his giving nature and ultimately fell in love with her earth angel—those who walk among us with an expressed purpose of showing us the way. Although he was twenty years her senior, she had met her soul mate and the only father her children would come to know and truly love. Little Anthony's prayers were finally answered!

The love and relationship of Mr. Z, Angelina, and her four children evolved, and the two decided to marry. To Angelina, Mr. Z offered stability, love, and the family structure they all so desperately sought. This happy family of six soon welcomed two new additions—little Paul and young Janet. Little Paul was born in 1935. He was big in stature and always in search of new and different paths to define him. Janet followed along in 1936. Revered by her siblings and friends, she was an unusual soul, always concerned for others and protective of her family. She lived her life as if each day were a gift to be cherished for the moment. They continued to live in a neighborhood that was categorized and governed by the streets—territory, power. Mr. Z and Angelina did all they could do to protect and teach their children the power of love and family unity. During their time together, many poignant and lasting life lessons were imparted by Mr. Z, and his sudden passing due to colon cancer (when Paul was eight and Janet seven) was a devastating loss for the family!

Paul used his acquired intelligence and inquisitive nature to seek out adventure and test the limits of life. As such, the public and private school systems could not capture his imagination, cultivate his energy, or recognize his inherent strength and competence. They merely accommodated him, leaving him to do tasks that utilized his mechanical mind and physical ability. At school, he could be found on any given day fixing furniture or doing maintenance work just to keep busy. The school administration did not realize that Paul was a diamond waiting to be polished!

Paul's energy was vast, and his mission was to find purpose, connection, and opportunities for meaningful contribution. The neighborhood streets offered him an attractive way to do so—territory, power, position—who owned what, who was connected to whom, who had access to what commodity. This young boy, who had lost his father at an early age, yearned for his return. He missed his role model of a man of character, conviction, and passion—someone Paul longed to become. He yearned for his mother's attention and gained "his stripes" deepened in a loss that no child should ever be forced to endure.

Life continued, and Paul created his status, his place as the toughest, most fearless, afraid of nothing and no one. Battles and physical triumphs created *his* place. Through this voyage, he "arrived," but that wasn't enough to satisfy Paul. He wanted something more, something he could not identify or find the right venue to attain. He unknowingly was in search of a future, *his* agenda and *his* place in the world.

The path he chose had taken a turn at the age of fourteen when his eyes embraced his future bride, Dorothy Teresia. Dorothy was a bright, ambitious young woman whose popularity and promise were what he longed for. Her family was stable, supportive, and well-grounded. Her life was filled with opportunity and purpose, as her family resided on the "other side of the tracks." At first sight, Paul knew Dorothy was intended to be in his life, and so his pursuit began. For Paul, this became a decisive pursuit; for Dorothy, an incidental annoyance!

The chance meeting of Paul and Dorothy occurred at the local roller-skating rink. It was a Saturday night, and the neighborhood youth convened for this weekly ritual. During this "date night out" session, all skaters played a game in which they were subject to a variety of infractions that put them into a phony jail, their only way out being another skater to pay bail and marry them. As Paul dutifully freed Dorothy, he placed a fake ring on her finger and made a vow that, in time, this would be for real! Dorothy inwardly thought that Paul was just a crazy fool and let the comment pass. Dorothy's life was a neat package, all focused and planned and reinforced by strong family roots and values. All the men in her life were refined and educated. In Paul's mind, Dorothy would be the complement to his life that he always sought after. Dorothy embodied the status and promise Paul pursued, and Paul embodied the spontaneity and zest for life that Dorothy unknowingly searched for. He would be her protector and strength!

Paul persevered, and Dorothy came to recognize the strength and ability of the man who captured her heart and imagination and the one who would come to define her future forever. Though their worlds were vastly different and their experiences foreign to each other, the love that evolved shielded any rejection of this marriage. In 1954, against the wishes of her family and friends, Paul and Dorothy began their new life together as husband and wife. This youthful love and blissful marriage at the age of eighteen masked the journey of challenges and triumphs they would come to know. As fate would have it, they were destined to be forever together.

Paul's sister, Janet, was so happy about their union and her newly designated sister. She continued to live her life close to her family but always maintained a premonition that she would not see her future beyond her high school years. This intuition was interpreted by some as superstition, and so life continued. Weeks before the end of the school year (just after her fifteenth birthday), Janet did something totally out of character. It is this mystery that happened one day in the city of Long Beach that left an indelible mark on our hearts forever.

It was a typical New York summer day. Janet, her cousin, and her cousin's boyfriend decided to walk along the shoreline of Atlantic Beach in Long Beach, New York. As witnessed by those on the boardwalk that day (some of whom were nuns living in the local convent), it was a sunny day that quickly turned to darkness. The sky exploded with lightning, the sea erupted, and Janet was whisked away by the riptide. All those on the beach remained dazed, staring at each other, unsure of what just happened. Suddenly, an eerie calm came over the seas and the sunshine returned…Janet was gone. She was found nine days later by a fisherman out at sea.

The family pondered the surreal experience of Janet's demise and strained to make sense of why she was taken from them at such an early age. The church was filled with people mourning the loss of this beautiful soul. Then, as if a sign from above, and to the amazement of all present that day, a bolt of lightning entered the room, hit the coffin, and the melody of birds singing filled the tabernacle. The songbirds were Janet's choir, the dome of nature now her church. On that day, heaven embraced an angel! It was at this time that Paul and his family realized that Dorothy was intended to enter their lives at this particular time to assume the role Janet once played in the life of the Zimmerman family.

As Janet would have had it, life went on. Paul's agility and uncanny strength always made him a natural athlete, and his tenacity challenged him to feats of greatness. As a forever Yankee fan, Paul actively pursued his dream of becoming a New York Yankee. Though called back for a position with the team, he was not able to pursue this journey. The Yankee farm team could not provide him with enough resources to support his impending family, and as always, Paul put them before his dreams. Instead, Paul became a truck driver, hauling large loads of wood and building supplies others feared to transport. His strength was unmatched and his limits undefined.

Soon after, Paul and Dorothy welcomed their firstborn child, Donna Maria. Dorothy, having a strong faith in the holy family, made a vow at this time that every daughter born to her family would bear some derivative of Mary in their name. Donna was a beautiful child and was welcomed and adored by all! Paul Jr., a happy, bouncing baby boy, followed two years later.

Life continued, and as the neighborhood deteriorated, everyone was moving out east to Long Island, New York. Angelina and her son Anthony declared first with the caveat that they would not leave Queens without Paul, Dorothy, Donna, and Paul Jr. With a third on the way, Paul and Dorothy decided to pool their resources and move into a new home, living with Angelina and Anthony. With mounting bills and added responsibility, Paul had to increase resources quickly. It was at this point that Paul discovered his vocation, or, shall we say, it discovered him!

To accommodate a growing family and space for both Angelina and Anthony, an extension needed to be added to their new Long Island home. They contracted the work to a licensed electrician since neither Paul nor Anthony had experience in this field. Although this contractor was difficult to understand due to a speech impediment, the family was confident in his competence. As they watched the contractor perform the work and became acclimated to his fastidious workmanship, Paul's industrious mind went into overdrive. Seizing the opportunity and capitalizing on his gift of gab (something the contractor did not possess), Paul came up with a proposal that would address his family's financial burdens and the contractor's speech impediment. He proposed that he would do the marketing for the contractor on consignment, and the contractor would do the job. The contractor happily agreed to the terms, and they soon landed a big project in the local village. The magnitude of this new project was so intimidating to the contractor that he left the job undone and was nowhere to be found. Paul was faced with two options—to quickly learn how to do electrical work and finish the job or fail. To Paul, this challenge was too attractive to do the latter. Paul, the child that the schools were unable to educate, applied himself diligently and quickly learned the electrical business. He became so proficient in the trade that he ultimately became a master licensed electrician, a title that men worked for many years to obtain.

Now with two children and great trade, life was good! Paul's vocation gave him status, security, and a chance at a viable future for himself and his family. It was unlike the life he had known in earlier years when the family lived moment to moment and addressed tomorrow when, and if, it came! Feeling the success of his business and enjoying it, Paul wasn't home much. He was always out and about, drumming up new business, as he completed the jobs at hand. Dorothy immersed herself into family life and was comforted by the love and support of Angelina and her extended neighborhood family. For Angelina, this was a second and destined chance to inculcate the life lessons she learned to her grandchildren. Angelina wholeheartedly loved them and treasured living with them. She considered Dorothy the daughter she tragically lost and always reminded her that she had to "make up" for what her son lacked in his absence while building up his business. In her mind, God had sent Dorothy to fill the void created by Janet's passing.

As the neighborhood grew, an extended family was born that included a close confidant and friend, Ruth Farrington. Ruth lived in the house across the street. Ruth and her husband, Dave, were the pioneers in the area, having built their own home while living with a child in a tent on the property. They were the first to move into the neighborhood even before the pavement of the streets! Ruth and Dorothy's friendship flourished and remained in full bloom for over fifty years until her passing in 2020! They had always been quite a team together, like Mutt and Jeff! Each afternoon, they would visit to share the tales of the day, comforting each other's sorrows or reveling in each other's happiness, nurturing and growing in love every day. There were many times when they had to put their heads together to solve life's dilemmas. Ruth was always the go-to advisor when a child was sick or wisdom needed to be imparted. When funds were short, it was Ruth and Dorothy who pooled their resources to make sure there was baby food and diapers. Together, many obstacles were overcome, and love was abundant.

Paul began acclimating himself to family life and found new ways to define his role. He longed to be needed and felt good about himself when others depended on him. In addition to work, he immersed himself in Little League Baseball, the local Farmingdale team. He quickly became a true hero to the young boys and their families and would come to be known throughout the community through his coaching over the years. At work, too, he became a role model and mentor for young men eager to learn the electrical trade, those who were lost in conflicts and in need of a life direction—similar to him.

As time passed, Paul and Dorothy settled nicely into their new life on Long Island.

Dorothy could be found many nights at the kitchen table with a cup of coffee and an old typewriter. It was during these moments that she would reflect on, translate, and capture the experiences of the day. Through the years, an anthology of writings chronicled family life at the Zimmerman home and gave voice to the myriad of experiences encountered.

The arrival of their third child, named Angela in honor of Angelina, the rock of the family, was welcomed with great happiness. Early on in life, Angela had several asthma attacks, pneumonia, and allergies. There were many trips to the hospital, several stays in the waiting room, and long nights of worry. On one occasion, pneumonia progressed so quickly in Angela that the doctors informed Paul and Dorothy that she may not survive. Moments of waiting turned into hours, and the potential loss of a child loomed over them like a dark cloud, a seeming eternity. Dorothy reflected on this experience in her writings. In "Where There Is Faith, There Is Love," she wrote:

> My head was in a distant fog and my thoughts were rambling on, as I was trying to keep in touch with reality to comprehend what was going on about me. I wanted to pray, to cry at the top of my lungs all at the same time, but I knew I must try to control the overwhelming emotions in my body. I prayed silently to the Lord, 'give Paul and me and our children the strength to accept Your will. Please, please, dear God, give us back our daughter.'
>
> My husband Paul and I had been waiting for what seemed an eternity in the hospital waiting room for news of our daughter. We had not spoken to each other for we were each lost in our thoughts. However, we both sensed how the other felt, and it seemed we were consoling each other with our silence.
>
> There was a continuous stream of doctors and nurses coming in and out of the elevator in their crisp, white, uniforms, and the smell of the hospital was in the air all around us. Each time one passed, we would look up hoping that this would be the one to bring us some news of Angela. Each time, however, they would walk briskly past us, going about their business. I could not help but wonder where they were all going in such a hurried place, while we were waiting here so patiently for some word. The hands on

the big clock on the wall just kept going around and around, and one hour slipped into the other, as our anxieties grew greater.

Just this morning, our little family of five had gotten up, as usual, to start our day. We were all very cheerful. It was Sunday and we all could enjoy a leisurely breakfast before going to church. Donna, the oldest child at the age of four, and Paulie, aged two were busily making plans with their father. We had just gotten a new movie camera and they were all excited about taking home movies for the first time. They couldn't wait to ham it up with their new baby sister, Angela, who was only four months old. Angela slept blissfully through all the confusion around her. Paulie proudly put on his cowboy outfit for his film debut and Donna made her grand entrance in her favorite party dress and high heels. It didn't bother her a bit that she was having difficulty walking in them. Of course, I dressed our littlest star in her frilliest outfit, too. Our movie-making began amid much laughter. My husband and I were particularly amused at the antics the children used to make their baby sister laugh. We commented, 'this is how stars are born.' I had noticed that Angela was having a bit of trouble breathing, and I thought to myself that she must have been getting a cold. It didn't seem bad enough to give it another thought at the time.

As the day went on, Angela was having more and more trouble breathing until, finally, it became a struggle for her. We immediately rushed her to the hospital for oxygen and a diagnosis of what was wrong. 'What could it be? Why was the doctor taking so long? Would she be all right?' Just as my rambling thoughts were bringing us near a mental collapse, our family doctor appeared. I knew in an instant, by the grim look on his face, that the news was not good. He tried to tell us as gently as possible, that our little Angela had double pneumonia and, because of her tender age, she might not survive. 'Oh, God! It seemed so unfair!' 'How could He give us this baby to love and then take her away so soon?' What anguish my poor husband and I were going through? He was trying to console me and pray aloud at the same time. This seemed more than we could bear.

We have had many problems in the past, both financially and otherwise, but my husband had always been so strong and had always managed to find a solution. Now, the sight of this big, strong man broken up just tore my heart in half. For a second, I almost forgot my grief. It was as though now all of our other problems were so minute. All that mattered was that we would be given the grace to have our daughter returned to us in good health.

The next three days were like a nightmare. I was aware of what was going on, but everything seemed so distant and disarranged. We were allowed to spend the days in Angela's hospital room. She was fighting for her life with each labored breath in her oxygen tent. Paul and I did a lot of praying, as we closely watched the movement of her chest with each gasp for air.

During our long vigil, I thought of many things. I thought about how foolish I had been wasting my time and energy worrying about our ever-present shortages of money and all the things we didn't have. If only I had taken the time to look around and thank God for all the good things that surrounded us. We had three beautiful children and a lovely home, which I could have enjoyed so much more if I hadn't been so full of self-pity. My husband started a business that was not doing so well at the time, but it was holding its own and fed and clothed us. Instead of being grateful for that, I was always looking for more. I resented the fact that there was so much housework and endless mounds of laundry, which I had to do by hand since we couldn't afford a washing machine. Someone else always seemed to have more than we had. I didn't realize then that it takes time and hard work to reach each goal, and those material things would come in time to those who had faith. I had never stopped pitying myself long enough to appreciate my extended family, especially my mother-in-law, who was always there to help with the housework and the children. Most of all, she always gave us love and encouragement to go on. She tried to convey to us her strong faith in the will of God. She was truly a beautiful person, so full of love and compassion for everyone and everything.

All through those three days of anxiously waiting for my daughter to regain her health, my mother-in-law stayed at our apartment to care for the other children and tend to the house-work. I knew her heart was also breaking with the thought of what might happen to our precious Angela. She wanted so badly to be with us in the hospital at Angela's cribside, but she knew she could be so much more helpful to us at home offering comfort to our other children who missed their baby sister so much. They loved their grandmother very much, and her very presence seemed to give them a sense of security in our absence. Every night, as we wearily came home with our eyes swollen with tears, my mother-in-law knew, without asking, that there was no change in Angela's health. She tried so hard to console and give us strength with her love and gentle words of encouragement, while she was at a point of exhaustion herself.

On the fourth day, before my husband and I entered the hospital fearing the worst, I suddenly realized that the sun was shining so beautifully, the birds were singing and that spring was in the air all around us. I prayed a silent prayer, 'God gives us one more chance. Make our baby well! You gave us the miracle of such a beautiful day; give us our daughter healthy once again.' We so wanted to teach her all the joys of living that I had so sadly forgotten over the past few years. We walked through the long corridor to Angela's hospital room. Our prayers were answered; the oxygen tent had been removed, and we knew, at a glance, that our baby would be well again. How gloriously happy we were. My husband and I wept openly in each other's arms. We thanked God and everything holy. We held Angela for the first time in four days. The feel of her little body cuddling in our arms made us forget all the worry of the last few, agonizing days.

That night, when we came home, our eyes were still swollen with tears; but this time, they were tears of happiness. Not only had my little daughter been saved, but also so had I. I vowed, silently, that I would never again cheat my little family and myself of all the wondrous joys of living. My dear mother-in-law said, 'God closes one door, but He always opens another.' I will always thank her for showing me the way, with her great faith and love. I feel that a door had been opened to me for a whole new outlook on life. I know now where there is faith, there is love, and that this is the greatest gift any mother can give her children. I hope that I too will be able to convey this to my children as the years go on.

Keeping this journal helped Dorothy get through many rough times in her life. With Angela saved and her life continuing, two more children, Janet and Mary, were born.

Suddenly, space was at a premium and the four-room-extension apartment became too small for their growing family. The children occupied their time playing hide-and-seek in the attic crevices that surrounded each room, in the limited closet space, and more often, in the backyard, weather permitting. They adjusted to the lack of space, but Paul and Dorothy knew they needed to move to a larger home. It was at this time that they met yet another milestone in their life.

After the birth of their fifth child, Dorothy and Paul were fortunate enough to discover that the house next door was being foreclosed, and they had the opportunity to purchase it. It was a great challenge to Paul, as it had been badly neglected by previous owners and was in complete disrepair. With assistance from the neighborhood family, courage, and imagination, they transformed this house into a home. From mangled walls, cracked floors, broken lights, and damaged appliances, this home was transformed! With his usual determination, skill, and fearless attitude, he was able to turn that house into the most beautiful home on the block. Angelina and Anthony were so happy that they were still within proximity to their family—about twenty feet!

Before long, Barbara, their sixth child, was born, and life progressed. Paul was working, the money went fast, and the future unfolded. With six children now, every day Dorothy was stretched to the limit. Although time was scarce," love was abundant, and family and neighborhood support were ever-present. She continued her journal writing each night into the early-morning hours. It was her time to reflect upon life's occurrences and add perspective to this dynamic existence. In "A Mother's Winter Dream," she lovingly recalls a day in the life of her little angels. It goes like this.

I reluctantly opened my eyes to see what the noise was all about so early in the morning and was petrified to see a gun pointed at me right between the eyes. In a quivering voice, I asked, 'who is it? what do you want?' I knew my husband had already left for work and I was ready to turn over the family fortune of $1.25 that I had in my wallet if they would just go away. 'All we want is breakfast mommy' came a tiny voice whose body was holding a toy pistol. By this time, I was a mass of jelly and relief. All I could manage to say was 'what a way to start a day,' and I dragged my weary bones down to the kitchen to make breakfast.

As my six darling little monsters sat down to eat their cereal, they held a conference and decided to award me a badge of bravery. At this point, I wasn't sure whether it was for something they had already done that might shock me or something that they were contemplating doing. By the end of the day, I would know why. In an almost pleading voice, I said, 'after breakfast, why don't you all go downstairs in the playroom and color for a while.' This seemed a good idea and down they went with Jennifer, our dog, following them. Ah, I thought, quiet at last, now I can have my coffee. 'Ma, Mommy, come down, Jennifer made.' I rolled up the newspaper I was about to read and went stomping down the stairs furiously. Child guidance books tell you not to hit children, but they don't say anything about not hitting naughty dogs. What a sight to behold at the bottom of the stairs, six little children cowering over one frightened dog. 'Mommy,' said my five-year-old, Mary, pleading with her big blue eyes, 'don't you always tell us to be kind to animals?' How could one softhearted mother win a case like this? So, I just went about the cleaning detail and then upstairs to try to have my cold coffee! Outside, there were endless mounds of snow. Could I survive another day in the house with six snowbound youngsters and one very timid dog?

It has been quiet for a while, too quiet! Once again, I went to investigate. The children were engaged in modern artwork. How beautiful it was. Too bad it was on the walls instead of paper! The sight of me clenching my teeth scared the children and they surrounded three-year-old Barbie, the culprit, to shield her from her 'big, bad mommy.' Their spokesperson, Mary, once again pleaded the case. 'She is only a baby and doesn't understand. Don't get mad at her, she is so little.' 'Yeah, I am only a baby, I don't understand… Don't get mad, I sorry,' Barbie volunteered, and she promptly gave me a bear hug that, of course, soothed my ruffled nerves. 'OK, sit down and watch television.' I began venting all my frustrations on the poor walls I was scrubbing.

This time, it was six-year-old Janet who said, 'we have to have lunch now.' 'What, it is only eleven o'clock, I said.' 'Mommy, we have to have lunch now. 'Bozo is having his on television, he asked us to join him.' Could anyone argue with Bozo?! So, we had lunch. After twelve sandwiches and four spills, we could finally settle down to an afternoon of fun and relaxation.

If you can't fight it, join it, so we all went out for some snow fun. This was not a very strategic move on my part, because outside they got reinforcements of about ten other little darling monster friends. With my son, Paul, age nine, and daughter, Angela, age eight, as commanding officers, they decided to attack the enemy; namely me! Being the cowardly enemy that I was, I retreated promptly only to fall into a drift of snow on top of my poor unsuspecting dog. One bloody nose coming up, mine! Donna, being ten years old, got a twinge of pity for her poor mom and called off the forces explaining, 'Mom must to be getting old, she is slipping.' I still haven't figured out whether she meant I was slipping on ice or my mind was slipping. We then called a truce. After all, hadn't I always taught them to be kind to elderly people? Besides, didn't they have to keep me in condition; who else could cook them supper?!

Next on the agenda, my little balls of energy and their reinforcements decided to build a snowman. After hours of hard labor, we had a big fat, cross-eyed snowman on our front lawn that they promptly labeled Mom! I decided to take this as a form of flattery. There aren't many people who can have a statue dedicated to them! After all, I didn't consider myself fat, only pleasingly plump, and my eyes only crossed when I clenched my teeth. It was now about the time when our hero, dad, would be home, so we all bid farewell to our neighborhood friends (and enemies) and our Snow Mom and advanced into the house to make supper with whatever energy I had left.

Have you ever tried to make supper with six hungry children and one dog invading the kitchen? One wanted hamburgers, one wanted franks, and so on. 'How about some nice hot chicken soup? It is good for you.' I said, trying to brainwash them. At this crucial moment, in walked dad. 'What did you do all day?' By this time, I was too tired to answer sanely, so I decided to stick to the Fifth Amendment. 'Guess what?' he said merrily. 'More snow is expected tonight.' All I could do was clench my teeth and cross my eyes, whereupon, he remarked, 'that snowman DOES bear a resemblance to you!'

When all the children were going to sleep that night, they asked the good Lord to bless daddy, mommy, and their dog. After all, daddy was their hero, mommy, their 'lackey' and the dog was their animal and they loved us all. This was very touching, but I didn't like the category they put me in. I attributed it to the innocence of youth. After all, they did say they loved me…

Later in the evening, as I sat quietly with that cup of coffee, I told Paul of a dream I had of moving to Australia. By this time, he figured I had flipped or needed some sleep and decided he had better humor me and asked me why. Very smugly, I answered, 'I heard it was summer there… I can dream, can't I?' 'Yes,' he said in earnest, 'but look at all the fun you would be missing!' This was the time for me to retreat to bed.

As I looked in on my little angels sleeping, I decided, I wouldn't trade places with anyone else in the world. Where else would I find such excitement and love at the same time? So, if I am going to go crazy, I might as well do it right here where I belong, and they understand me…

Dorothy's sense of creativity and purpose captured the imagination of her children. When resources were low, this attribute created many wonderful childhood memories—long walks in the woods (snowball fights too!), crafts, and community carnivals to support a variety of charities. It was not uncommon to spend summer days preparing for a day-long fundraiser to address muscular dystrophy. Neighbors were asked to bake, then purchased their own goods at the bake sale; all the pets were corralled for a petting zoo that neighbors were charged admission to attend, and children practiced their respective musical talents for a sing-along that all paid a nominal fee to attend. All proceeds went to support Jerry's Kids and were proudly donated during the annual Labor Day telethon for muscular dystrophy hosted by Jerry Lewis. Their home was truly "mother-full" and, even in the most difficult times, their family was rich in faith and love. They learned these values early and hold these memories forever.

When Paul's business was booming, the money flowed, and life was easier. With six children and a home, however, resources were stretched to the limit. Many times, when the business was slow, the next meal was a question mark, the phone remained unanswered, as the bill collectors called, and painful times remembered. However, Paul was still in search…to do it better or sometimes not at all. There were periods when he did not work. These "vacations" lasted until moments of great desperation when the house was at imminent risk of foreclosure, vehicles repossessed, electricity turned off, and the calls from creditors abounded. It became a normal course of life— the ebbs and flows of our childhood reality. Having Angelina right next door was always a source of comfort to Dorothy during these times. Angelina's influence extended throughout the neighborhood. Her coffee pot was always full, and her table was open for daily visitors. She was always lovingly referred to as Grandma by all. She was extremely overprotective, dutifully watching from her window each time her grandchildren rode a bike or played with the other children in the neighborhood in front of the house. In one incident, Angelina made Paul go with Donna on an overnight Girl Scout camping trip, *across the street!* In her day, young ladies did not stay away from home without an escort. Her resourcefulness and nurturance were always felt, and many stories of her character continue to be told to this day.

One of the family's favorite recounts of Angelina occurred when she had to gather up loose change to purchase a jar of baby food. Another small family crisis—Paul Jr.'s pajamas were tattered beyond repair, and after hearing of it, Angelina's sharp mind went to work yet again to solve this predicament. That afternoon, she summoned Dorothy and the children to her home—as she did each day. When they arrived, she showed them a box on the table holding a welcome surprise for Paul Jr. As he opened it, he found flowered pajamas. Believing that young men don't wear flowers, he questioned why his grandmother would purchase them on his behalf. She immediately declared that these were special Hawaiian pajamas, made especially for him. Needless to say, he wore them pridefully for some time to come. When Dorothy questioned Angelina, she pointed toward her back door and quickly declared that she no longer needed the curtains! These are among the many tales of courage, imagination, hope, frustration, and pain to be later reflected on as we all experience being in the waiting room, anticipating the fate Paul was to endure.

The family continued to grow and learn from each other. Donna, the eldest child, set a wonderful example to her younger siblings in school and at home; she was the pioneer. Paul, the only son, was truly industrious, mowing lawns, shoveling snow, and earning money at an early age. Angela was always the daydreamer, whose imagination was only exceeded by deep curiosity and support of the underdog. Janet loved the harmony and always removed herself from family conflict, oftentimes retreating into the playpen. Mary, the fifth child in our family tree, was the virtuous one who always exemplified our best family values, and finally, Barbara was intelligent and possessed endurance as the youngest of six.

Through it all, we always survived together, drawing upon each other's support, love, and encouragement. Throughout childhood, we always understood the value of family and the fundamental connections that would always be our constant.

The seasons passed, winter came, and with it a shortage of work for Paul's business. Money was in very short supply. The mortgage was three months behind, and foreclosure proceedings began. Our family home was listed in the newspaper, but as a family, we couldn't imagine being anywhere else—this was *our* home. Each evening, our small ears listened to adult discussions filled with great anxiety and hopelessness. Then, the industrious Paul Jr. presented a resolution, an envelope with cash he had earned in previous years mowing lawns and shoveling snow. The mortgage was paid with funds he had saved for what seemed to him as forever! He was our hero of the moment and remains so to this day! In reflecting on those times, our family drew on our greatest assets, love and hope, for it was then that many life lessons were learned, and the interdependence of our family was understood and cherished.

These qualities ingrained in our family from the very beginning exemplified those principles near and dear to Angelina's heart. Although Angelina was always the problem solver of our family, throughout our childhood, she had many bouts with illnesses—diabetes, glaucoma, cataracts, and so forth. She was always afraid of dying and spent a great deal of time talking about the variety of ailments she was encountering. The year was 1967, and Angelina awoke in severe pain that necessitated a trip to the hospital. In fear of a tragic loss, her children remained in the waiting room of the hospital and, we, in the waiting room of our young minds at home. She, too, had a premonition that her days were limited and did her best to reconcile and find peace with her family and, ultimately, her Creator.

Paul arrived home with the depth of loss sketched all over his face and heaviness in his heart. We knew the outcome of his stay in the waiting room and the event that occurred on August 19, 1967. In the end, Angelina's kidneys failed, and she was once again joined with her soul mate, Mr. Z, and her daughter, Janet, in eternity. Her spirit soared in all of us, and we continue to feel the angel that we called Grandma on our shoulders, in our memories, and our hearts.

Just one week before her passing, Angelina had given Angela a beautifully wrapped box for her September birthday. When asked why she was giving it to her before her actual birth date, she indicated that she would not be there to celebrate, as Angelina sensed her time on earth was running out. Inside the package was a coveted Sinclair radio. Angelina's ingenuity and the use of Green Stamps always allowed her to obtain many meaningful gifts she could not otherwise have afforded to give. However, in her life and passing, she would never realize the abstract gifts of strength, love, and laughter she had bestowed upon her family and the impact that has had and will continue to have on them as they face the uncertain future. To the family, she was a "*shero*" leaving her indelible mark. Her life mattered, and she always played an integral role in shaping the character and values of her greatest treasure, her family!

In reflecting on the life of Angelina, even to this day, we draw courage from her tenacity and resilience. Many stories can be told of these characteristics, and one in particular remains with us.

It was about a time when Paul and Dorothy were both hospitalized, and the authorities arrived at Angelina's doorstep to take her grandchildren into temporary custody for care in their parents' absence. Armed with a broom, Angelina proceeded to declare to the caseworker that she would care for them, and they were not to be taken anywhere! When further confronted, she chased this individual down the block, never to be heard from again. As children, we could not imagine our grandmother running so fast in her house duster and knee-high stockings rolled down around her ankles!

Angelina loved abundantly and always had a story at the ready. Holidays were marked with special foods, favorite stories, songs, and animated conversation. Guests left with their appetites satisfied and their hearts full. We always knew and felt her unconditional love, and these stories remind us of the depth and value of family in this chaotic world. Another loss, another void, as time waits for no one.

Shortly after the tragic loss of their beloved Angelina, Dorothy and Paul suffered yet another. Dorothy's father lost his battle with colon cancer, leaving the family mentally and physically fatigued from his full year of treatment. It was during this time that Paul redeemed himself with Dorothy's family (as they had started their marriage with less than mutual family blessings). The love and compassion Paul exhibited were unsurpassed. He so admired his father-in-law and did everything humanly possible to care for and comfort him as his days became limited. It was so ironic that both Dorothy and Paul's fathers lost their lives due to colon cancer. Paul was once again in the waiting room, witnessing the deterioration of yet another important male role model in his life. In doing so, he helped Henry's last days be marked with dignity and his passing with grace.

With Henry now at eternal rest, Dorothy's mother, Berta, was forced to live alone. The death of her husband was devastating, as this was not the life order she anticipated as her destiny. After countless and almost lethal heart attacks, she always believed that *she* would be greeting Henry in heaven. She continually declined Paul and Dorothy's countless offers to live with them and their six children on Long Island. It was felt that Berta's nerves couldn't bear the daily life of this big family. Each time she babysat her grandchildren, Paul and Dorothy were anxiously greeted at the door on their return. She soothed her nerves with a cup of warm milk and the quiet of her own home. She truly preferred to stay at home in Jamaica, Queens, and reassembled her life there. As Henry had lived a focused and purposeful life, she was left with adequate resources to do so. Each Sunday, Paul, Dorothy, and the grandchildren devotedly visited, and phone calls were frequent to help fill the void Berta felt as each day passed.

After years of being independent, Berta succumbed to her loneliness and decided it was time to open her heart to a companion. Through her social network, she met Louie, an Italian immigrant who had lost his wife years earlier. The two dated and married shortly thereafter. Berta was reserved about the details of this relationship, neither complaining nor rejoicing. She continued to do part-time work to support the household as Louie felt it "beneath him" to do so. Louie had five children from his previous marriage, and many were estranged (explanation unknown at the time). Dorothy's heart was not comfortable with the companion taken by Berta. Another premonition was revealed to the family—ill feelings toward Louie not based on fact but intuition. How was he truly treating their beloved mother? Was she happy? In the company of family, all appeared well—but was it? There was something unnerving and uncomfortable about him. His eyes were empty, his manner stoic, and his responses controlled. As a family, we found it was impossible to get close to him. Even Fritz, our German shepherd, growled at him and promptly relieved himself on Louie's leg!

It was an October evening, 1969. The children were in bed, and Dorothy received the call she always dreaded but knew was inevitable. Her intuition was usually right on target, and sad to say, this time was no exception. The caller gurgled and immediately hung up. Thinking it was a prank, Dorothy returned to sleep. The next morning, she awoke to a call from Louie telling her that her mother went missing. For thirteen days and nights, local ponds were dredged, woods searched, and countless people interviewed. Berta had vanished without a trace or reasonable explanation. Once again, our family found themselves in the waiting room! Question marks arose when Berta's glasses were found still lying on her night table, as she was dependent on them. "How can she have gone somewhere without being able to see?" was the question in Dorothy's and Paul's mind. Why was her wedding ring left behind? What motivated her to leave her home? Questions, questions, questions; but alas…no answers to be found!

Dorothy and her only sibling, Henry, had such strong premonitions that Berta had never left the house. Henry, Dorothy, and Paul met and began a search for their missing mother. They felt that the police department was not doing enough to find Berta, so they decided to do their investigation. Louie was out on his daily visit to a family member when the three children took advantage of the opportunity to search Berta's home for clues of what happened. The quick search revealed her pocketbook and dentures still in their place, untouched. Time was running out, as Louie was due home shortly. Then, an intuition, driven by unknown energy, motivated Henry, Dorothy, Paul, and Henry's wife, Connie, to enter the family basement. As they pulled aside an area rug that traditionally lay beneath the dining table, the mystery unfolded. To their horror, there was evidence of newly poured cement, not quite dry. In sheer desperation, they began to dig with objects they found throughout the basement. Then, as they dug deeper, a distinctive odor filled the house, an odor that sent horror through their bodies…the odor of rotting flesh!

Dorothy and Paul grew increasingly alarmed and felt that the police should now be contacted to report the anticipated location of Berta's body. As they frantically reported their suspicions to the officer who answered, they could immediately feel his disbelief through the telephone line. He then, very coldly and abruptly, told them to call back when the body was truly discovered. In his mind, they were just hysterical, and their need to find their mom was making them imagine the worst! In the moments that followed, the smell deepened, and with greater certainty, Dorothy was positive that her mother was found. In a great sense of urgency, she and Paul left the house and ran directly to the police department, their speed motivated by the fear that Louie would be home soon, and they could be his next victims. They reported the incident once again to the department, hoping that their presence would prompt them to listen. A kind detective from the burglary department agreed to return to the home in an unofficial capacity, as a friend, to investigate since none of the other officers would comply for lack of evidence.

As the officer entered the home, it became apparent to him that what was uncovered were indeed human remains, and he immediately summoned homicide to have an official investigation finally initiated. All the major news networks and publications reported on this event with much public debate, and the prime suspect, Louie, was brought to trial for the death of Berta. The account Louie told was unbelievable and a grave injustice to the legacy of a woman who was small and frail in stature and had a life filled with medical sufferings. Emigrating from Germany as Hitler established himself and the Nazi regime, experiencing life-threatening heart attacks and the like—for someone to take her life now after she overcame all these atrocities! Louie's account of events leading up to Berta's "disappearance" went something like this…Louie claimed that on that October evening, he and Berta were enjoying soup for their dinner meal. Louie, always being critical of Berta's cooking, complained that the soup had a metallic taste to it and testified that she was trying to poison him. He became physically violent toward Berta and caught her in a choke hold, trying to force her to admit to his allegations. His physical strength became too much for frail Berta, and her body succumbed to the strangulation. Not knowing what to do, he decided it would be best to hide her body and make up the story of her disappearance.

Of course, a different account was given by the prosecution. Weeks before the murder, coffee cans filled with dirt were seen being tossed out from the basement window each day. Autopsy reports indicated that Berta's dentures, jewelry, and glasses were removed and lye placed in her makeshift grave to hasten the decomposition of the body—the evidence—grounds for premeditation. Louie's plans were interrupted when Berta's children desperately searched for answers. Although Louie was convicted of premeditated murder due to the overwhelming evidence against him, it was to the dismay of the family and the disbelief of all present in the courtroom, that the judge issued Louie probation. It was the opinion of the court that incarceration would not be an option for a man of seventy-two years of age, as he was not well enough to survive any other disposition. To the recollection of Berta's family, it was the first time in the State of New York that such a sentence was issued for premeditated murder. In their hearts and minds, the outcome of the trial became *their* sentence for the rest of *their* lives. Questions ran rampant… Why would someone hurt Grandma? How could the court have been so lenient? The truth remained in Berta's decomposed body and Louie's conscience. Plans were completed for Berta's funeral posthaste, and a somber celebration paid tribute to her life and legacy. After the burial, Dorothy and Henry set out to settle the financial affairs of their poor, departed mother. They arrived at Berta's bank to gather her papers and empty her safety deposit box. To their surprise, instead of money or important documents, the box was filled with play money wrapped in a stocking with traces of dirt throughout. Although there were many speculations, to this day, the mystery remains unsolved.

Processing this horrific event as children was one of our greatest challenges. It became a very powerful life moment that would always distinctly reflect that time and experience. Certainly, our peers in suburbia couldn't or wouldn't understand, as it appeared so far from *their* reality, and it was something we did not openly discuss. It was a significant family loss and, undoubtedly, the most poignant one we will ever be forced to endure. With a closed casket, memories of Berta and visions of our last visit with her remain forever in the heart of each one of us. As children, experiencing this type of event made us feel *different*, as it was not a common occurrence among our peers, and we did not allow them to relate to it. It immediately became a family secret. Items that Berta once gave us became extremely important, as they tangibly connected us to her. One item, in particular, a cross that was blessed by the Pope, was a special reminder to us of Berta's grace and powerful faith. To our complete horror, this precious item was inadvertently left in a doctor's office dressing room when it was taken off during an annual exam. That loss opened the wounds of losing our dear grandmother all over again.

Ironically, some of our most difficult experiences can often be recollected or connected to songs that forever mark that time. One song's lyrics, in particular, that remained vivid was "I can see clearly now, the rain is gone…I can see all obstacles in my way… Gone are the dark clouds that had me blind…" Though we could not see the "rainbow I've been praying for," or the "bright, bright, bright sun-shiny day…" that song always left us with a sense that someday we could heal from the tragic times that have plagued our family.

It is a difficult process to lose someone at the hand of another's viciousness, then gracefully place him or her in the hands of God. In the aftermath, visions of seeing Louie's face in public places made us want to clench our fists and be ready to attack, just to realize that it was just another innocent stranger. The look of indescribable pain in our mother's eyes left us all numb inside. That look of the emptiness of losing someone special in our lives left us feeling so helpless and unable to comfort our poor, suffering mother. It was a massive challenge for us to make sense of this brutal murder, for none existed… just one big question mark. Many say that when the spirit is released from someone who dies at the hand of others, it travels for some time until it can rest in peace. All of us have come to know that spirit now. Berta's strength and courage are poignantly remembered, embraced, and will mark this sequence in our lives forever. Added to our pain, and as if a knife were pushed deeper into our hearts, it was alleged that while on probation, Louie left the United States and found a new bride in Italy, only to return and start a new family life. Justice? All of us are heartened by our conviction that justice will be realized on the ultimate of judgment days. In later years, each of us became committed to the notion of justice in our unique ways—in the community, in our family, workplace—innate to our character and tempered by yet another tragic experience in the waiting room.

Dorothy found solace in her family and started writing again. Her sadness poured into nightly recordings in her journal. It was a cathartic expression of experiences and emotions, just enough to allow her to greet the next day truly anew. In an "Open Letter to Mama" she wrote:

> As I sit here by the fireplace, watching the beautiful vibrant colors of the flames casting dim, fleeting shadows on the wall, my thoughts turn to you. Cuddled in my rocking chair, drinking in the warm cozy atmosphere, my mind drifts back to my childhood and our home, a home in which there was so much love and happiness. Many times, in my adult years, there were things that I had come to understand. How often I would have liked to sit down with you and talk about them, but I never took the time nor could I find the proper words to express my overwhelming feelings. Now as I take my pen in my hand, the words just seem to flow as my mind reminisces.
>
> You always spoke of the great happiness you experienced the day I was born and of the love a mother feels for a child. I could never comprehend this until I had the very same joyous experience the day my first daughter was born. I realized then that all you have done for me was done with a love that only a mother could feel for her child. I now know how happy you must have been the first time I smiled at you, the feel of

my first tooth, my first step, and, most of all, the thrill of hearing me say 'Mama' for the first time.

The most cherished memories I will ever have were the warm colorful ways we celebrated holidays. This was always the time when the spirit of love and giving prevailed and we were all so happy just being together with our family and friends. On Easter morning, I would get up and scamper through the house in my childish way, looking for the Easter basket that you had hidden with care during the night. How happy I was when I found the basket which was filled with candy and all the goodies that children love. Our visit from Santa Claus was an occasion that we all looked forward to for months in advance. We decorated our tree with care and the air was filled with excitement and anticipation. It got rather noisy at times when we all sang around the tree and opened our gifts with shrills of delight. How proud you were when your family all sat down to eat the dinner that took you days to prepare. You always made sure before we ate that we thanked the good Lord for all the blessings we had received and we did receive many, but the biggest blessing was you, dear Mama, you are the very heart of our family.

How vividly I remember waking up each morning to the smell of your bacon and eggs and the sound of your voice singing as you go about your chores of making breakfast. As I opened my eyes one morning, the sun was shining brightly through the window and it seemed that the branches of the trees were swaying in time to your song. I could not help but think, what a beautiful way to start a day.

Our house was always full of surprises. One of the most memorable was when I got my first pair of roller skates. I had wished so long and so hard for them and I couldn't wait to try them on. In my excitement, I fell almost immediately and hurt myself. You gently wiped away my tears and the touch of your lips made all the hurt go away. Only you could do this for me.

Do you remember the first time I wore lipstick, my graduation, and my first dance? Do you remember how you looked forward to each of these occasions almost as if they were milestones in your own life?

Our house in those years was always filled with my friends and laughter and music, as we all got together for our dancing session. We always found a cake on the old kitchen table that you baked with such loving care. This was only one of the reasons why you were 'Mama" for all my friends.

My mind reminisces further about a big event in my life, my wedding day. This was a day of mixed emotions. I was happy that I was about to embark on a new life with a man whom I loved and cherished, but after all the festivities were over, we both felt a twinge of sadness because we were to be separated. I came to realize later that we could never be separated. As long as I have my memory, you would always be with me and I would always be able to recall your wisdom to guide me and your love to comfort me.

You have taught me many things, for which I am grateful, and you have given me many gifts for which I am thankful; but the greatest gifts you have given me are the gifts of life and then the gift of faith to sustain me through life. My faith has given me the strength to accept whatever trials and disappointments fate may send my way. It has taught me to accept these trials and disappointments as the Will of God. It has also taught me the joys of living. I try to live each day to the fullest and enjoy all the good things God has given us. I shall never stop marveling at all the wonders of nature around us. So few of us have ever taken the time to notice the sun, the stars, the birds, the trees and the grass, the abstract images of the clouds each day. The list goes on endlessly; when you have an inner faith, you realize that God must love us to send us all these miracles and how beautiful life is. Thank you, dearest Mama, for giving me this faith, my life, hope, and happiness.

The fire grows dim in the fireplace; the shadows on the wall have stopped their dancing as the night descends upon us. As I close my heavy eyelids and enter into a contented sleep, I whisper a word of thanks to God for blessing me with my children, entrusting in me lives to love, mold, and guide down life's road. I also thank God for giving me to you dear Mama, for you are my inspiration, my guide, and my model. With a grateful and heavy heart…your loving daughter, Dorothy Teresa.

Paul always did what he could to comfort Dorothy now more than ever. Neither words nor actions could do much to fill the horrific void Dorothy felt. Only time tempered the pain, this misery that became yet another haunting chapter in our family history. Dorothy did not speak about it much as this pain was too deep and unknown. She received solace in the living—her family. It was not until years later when she dreamt of her mother and awoke comforted, with the realization that her mother made it "home" and was now at peace. To fill the void of Sunday visits with Grandma, Paul did what he could do to create family time. With limited resources, he would gather the children in the car, put his finger in the air, and take the family for drives in the direction of the wind. These are the times we remember, not knowing where we are going but happy to be doing it together. And so another chapter ends.

Fast forward! The time is now April 2004. Dorothy and Paul arrived at what they thought was an awards luncheon for a dear friend of the family, Ann. (This was not an unusual occurrence as Ann was a champion for children and families, and despite her humility her acts of kindness did not go unnoticed!) To their amazement, it was a surprise party celebration honoring their fiftieth wedding anniversary! Paul and Dorothy's children diligently worked to plan this special day for their beloved parents. Family and friends served witness as this beautiful couple renewed their vows and love for each other. Fifty years of life's ups and downs were faced together, hand-in-hand. What a blessing! It was at this time and in this moment that they reflected on their lives in the context of a lifetime of connections—friends and generations of family—their children, spouses, and fourteen grandchildren. The eyes are truly the windows of the soul. As they looked into each other's eyes, a lifetime of memories flooded their hearts and minds, memories of lives they have touched and molded in anticipation of a legacy to later behold. Lives that, in time, taught them many lessons about living in the waiting room. An abundance of memories…too many to tell. Where has the time gone? The following are just a few of those life moments that left quite an indelible mark and provided many a test of faith.

It was a typical spring afternoon and all the neighborhood children were returning from school in anticipation of an afternoon of play. Paul came home from work early this day and must have been destined to do so. One block from home, he witnessed a garbage truck careening into a small Volkswagen. After colliding, the car landed on its side, engulfed in flames with a young man trapped inside. Looking in the car, Paul and another neighbor knew time was short and immediate action was required to save this unfortunate young victim. With no time to spare, Paul mustered all of his strength, flipped the car over, and pulled the teenager to safety. Paul's heart was filled with happiness in knowing that he had made the difference between life and death for this young man. He was saved and, in essence, Paul was also saved. To acknowledge his heroism, he received the Carnegie Hero Award by the Carnegie Foundation, a very prestigious award acknowledgment.

Yet another memory etched in our minds was the family's pilgrimage to Yankton, South Dakota. It was there that the family was to reconnect with Dorothy's aunt, Tanta Regula, a Benedictine nun who was Berta's oldest sister and one of the founding members of the Sacred Heart Convent. Tanta Regula emigrated to the United States from Germany during the time of the Hitler regime. Joining a group of sixteen nuns, she created her legacy. Her contribution to the convent and her community was as the convent gardener. The convent spread hope and opportunity throughout the rural communities that surrounded their home, particularly at the local Native American Indian reservations. As their vision evolved, the convent grew. A school and hospital were soon added, allowing this community to become quite formidable in the Midwest education, health, and human service arena. It was during this visit that we, as children, experienced firsthand the joy of giving of ourselves unconditionally!

Each of us contributed our time and talents to Native American Indian children at the local reservations, embracing their culture and assisting them with their studies. It was truly this pilgrimage of charity that remains in our fondest memories to this day! This feeling and longing we all continually pursue allow us to go beyond ourselves and touch the hearts of so many. We have learned that in doing so, we are ourselves enriched. In the midst of all the charitable works Tanta Regula did, she had struggled through a battle with breast cancer for many years. After the shock and sorrow of her sister Berta's passing, her cancer came out of remission and rapidly took her life, leaving a tremendous void in ours once again. Yet another chapter in the Zimmerman family history.

And so life continued, and the children of Dorothy and Paul grew up tempered by the many lessons learned throughout their childhood.

Donna, their eldest, married Robert and had three sons. Robert Jr. is an electrician, Matthew a welder, and Nicholas, their youngest, works on nuclear submarines. Donna works with special needs children in a local school district in Virginia and has continued to pursue her education with an exceptional grade point average. As the eldest, her wisdom and leadership had always provided light in the darkest moments. She was the first and only sibling who moved out of state but always remained close in the hearts of the family she left behind.

Paul Jr. married Marietta and had four children. Paul Jr. had an active and productive career as a United States Marine Corps, second generation, and has retired from the Long Island Railroad. Their eldest, Jeanette, is married to George, has two children, and owns a very successful flower shop. Paul III is a decorated marine, has two sons, and just retired from the Long Island Railroad. Stephanie is a registered nurse, and Rebecca currently works for the Long Island Railroad. Paul Jr. had the arduous role of being the only son, constantly striving to be the best he could be.

Angela actively dedicated her life and career to health and human services to contribute to those in need. Although she never married, she remained an influence in the lives of many children, especially her nieces and nephews. As the middle child, she had always "marched to the beat of her drum," truly driven by the notion that all children deserve the opportunity to feel the magic of an enriching childhood, celebrated memories, and an embracing community. She is currently the director of development and alumni relations and teaches at Molloy University, Rockville Centre.

Janet married John and had four children. Melissa is an entrepreneur with one daughter, Jackie is a special education teacher with one daughter, Kelley has one son and works in the finance department of a car dealership, and Johnny is a Suffolk County police officer with one son. Janet works at a monument company where she has been for some time and takes great pride in her children and their accomplishments. As one of six children, any time there was a conflict, Janet continually "sought cover." Although she has outgrown that now, she always seeks peace and harmony in her household and world.

Mary was married to Michael and has two children, Michael Jr. and Anthony. Michael Jr. is an oceanic engineer who graduated from the Webb Institute of Naval Architecture and Anthony oversees pharmacological research after attending Northeastern University. Mary has had a long and substantial career working for a local school district and at the local library serving the community. She has invested much of her life in affording her children every opportunity to succeed, and they certainly have. As she cultivated her own family, these values remain her legacy to this day.

Barbara married Daryl and had one child, Sarah. Sarah is the youngest of fourteen grandchildren and is about to begin her career working with young children. As the youngest, she is always in a position of being a "little fish in a big pond." She is very intelligent and quizzical with a bright future of promise ahead of her. Barbara is a licensed massage therapist and has had a long and rewarding career.

All the siblings have contributed greatly to their respective communities and have always exhibited great empathy and sensitivity toward children and families who have experienced many of the same challenges that they have learned to endure.

Truly, the years preceding their fiftieth wedding anniversary were filled with many firsts for Dorothy and Paul; that is, the first wedding of the eldest grandchild, Jeanette, to George; three generations of proud marines; grandchildren's attendance at pre-K and college. The family was full, and the circle of love created and multiplied as we prepared for the next chapter in our lives.

Paul continued to work in his electrical trade, and Dorothy started her second career at a local child care agency. There, children came to know her love and character and affectionately referred to her as Miss Dottie. They, too, felt the abundant compassion of this phenomenal woman, who blessed the lives of so many despite the challenges she endured and the tests she had yet to face. Paul and Dorothy remained fairly healthy aside from hypertension and diabetes until another obstacle created a barrier in their lives.

It was August 2005, and Paul's doctor decided that the prolonged anemia he was experiencing needed to be further explored. Blood tests were administered, and a bone marrow biopsy was recommended. Upon completion of the tests, it was determined that Paul had myelodysplastic syndrome (MDS), preleukemia, something that would require regimens of blood tests, chemotherapy, and periodic transfusions for the rest of his life—another life moment.

MDS is a disease with the median age of onset at seventy. Often diagnosed as anemia, this insidious disease produces abnormal cells from the marrow that, in a moment, can become leukemia. One of the first family tasks was to become educated, empowered with enough information to understand, integrate, and ask questions. Knowledge is power! In that quest, a great deal of information was discovered.

Unfortunately, Paul had a severe case that prompted grueling regimens of chemotherapy every twenty-eight days as his only treatment option. With other health complications, he was not a candidate for a bone marrow transplant, which could have put him into complete remission. Once again, the family was in crisis, and once again, the family values of cohesion, unity, and unconditional love came forward to shepherd him through this new journey. On a rotating basis, all of us took turns—transfusions, monthly regimens of chemotherapy, blood tests, countless hours in the waiting room in anticipation, the confusion of integrating this new experience and the anticipated requirements of this journey untold.

It is interesting how families cope with different challenges. Hearing the words *myelodysplastic syndrome* and *chemotherapy* gives rise to the question, how much time remains? The transfusions and uncertainty, nausea, depression, and all of us in the waiting room, anticipating the future while reconciling the past, were overwhelming. It was during that time that we truly held on to every moment of today. Throughout the first year, this regimen became our ritual, and every blood test was a milestone on this journey. As part of a drug protocol, we were medically in uncharted waters looking for the key to arrest this insidious disease. In reflecting on this time, all of us, including Paul, went through a period of mourning due to the gradual loss of his health and physical agility, some of the core things that had so defined him through his years. It's hard to explain, but as he transitioned through this process, we missed him—who he was—then slowly began to adapt to the changing circumstances that made him so painfully reliant and truly in need of all of us. It was no accident.

Paul's diabetes continued to wreak havoc on his kidneys. BUN tests, potassium check, kidney function levels, doctor visits, and again, we're in the waiting room. Fifty percent functioning and holding 40 percent, it was at that point that the doctor recommended an access port be placed, as time was growing nearer to the dreaded dialysis machine. Constant checkups and blood tests—the kidneys at 33 percent and holding. Dialysis, another challenge and opportunity to reflect on life, the past, the future, today. When you hear the word *dialysis*, the fear of life being limited is imminent. It is truly these moments that make us realize our mortality. They are our milestones—life moments that we will recall for the rest of our lives. Now it's time to prepare, to have the access port put in. Time after time, it is postponed due to an unrealistic illusion that perhaps the kidney functioning would miraculously return. Twenty percent and holding, the time is getting closer to renal failure, the very thing that took the life of our sweet Angelina. Reflections in the waiting room became more serious as the challenges mount. Fourteen percent and holding! Six months were needed for the access port to mature enough to endure dialysis; it was now time.

The operation was successful and, as a family, we waited for the inevitable. Emotions were mixed between relief that it had been completed and hope that perhaps it would never be used. Dialysis? What would this come to mean? The family regrouped once again, as we faced this incredible new chapter in the life of the Zimmerman family. Paul gradually became weaker, his spirits down and his physical strength diminished. He could no longer work, no money, no savings, and the future in tremendous doubt. Dorothy could no longer maintain her job as she loyally accompanied Paul to each medical visit and patiently remained in the waiting room.

It was throughout this time that faith, love, and a sense of hope became a foundation for survival and the only thing we had to hold on to. Though Paul could not work, he always felt a need to continue his contribution to his community service program. As a thirty-year volunteer for Toys for Tots Program, a U.S. Marine Corps program that collected and distributed toys to children throughout the holiday season, Paul remained as active as he could be until his demise. When able, he could be found on the telephone corralling his senior citizen network to volunteer to support this program throughout the metropolitan region. It was a critical time for Toys for Tots, as many of the marine reservists who had ordinarily taken a lion's share of this responsibility were rapidly being deployed to Iraq. Paul always felt good about this work, and it rewarded him in more ways than even he realized. It certainly brought him back to the times when he was able to sponsor holiday celebrations for children who were terminally ill. He always had a soft spot for children. Some of us think that he tried to make the world a bit easier for children he encountered, particularly after the childhood experiences that he had endured. In a sense, he was a "catcher in the rye."

The Time Has Come

Any transition serious enough to alter your definition of self will require not just small adjustments in your way of living and thinking, but a full-on metamorphosis.

—Martha Beck, O Magazine,
Growing Wing, January 2004

Life moved forward for Paul, Dorothy, and their beautiful family. Paul's nausea began, the kidney function numbers continued to fall, and the inevitable finally occurred. On October 17, 2006, the call to a very despondent family was received—"go to the hospital." The family scurried; it was time. Paul was in renal failure, and there were no further options. Dialysis was now mandatory, and life once again took another turn, a true test of our inner strength and stamina. We all convened in the waiting room. It was one o'clock in the afternoon, and the nephrologist arrived. The kidneys were no longer functioning, and the body was becoming increasingly toxic. The choice at this point was to receive dialysis or die. Dialysis would now be our new reality, the new lifeline—each Tuesday, Thursday, and Saturday… forever!

On October 25, 2006, Paul was discharged from the hospital to the care of the "Anywhere" Dialysis Center. It is through the witnessing of events and testimonies from the unsung heroes here that we have come to know and integrate many powerful and sustained life lessons. The names are unimportant, but the messages are poignant. Through these experiences, we understand that every life that touches ours has meaning and purpose if we allow these lessons to enter our hearts and fuel our spirits. It is in this place that many life experiences, perspectives, and histories come to tell a story. It is uncommon but a familiar place where everyone is equal and the common denominator the same. It is here that we are together, in the waiting room.

WHATEVER YOU DID FOR
ONE OF MY LEAST BROTHERS
OR SISTERS, YOU DID FOR ME.
(MATTHEW 25:40)

Vignettes from the Waiting Room

The First Day

> People only see what they are prepared to see.
>
> —Ralph Waldo Emerson

It was the first day of a new routine, the first day at dialysis. We established a schedule; Paul would never be alone. Greeted with a smile, we were walked into the center and took our place among the other courageous recipients. We were new, and the anxiety and naivete showed on our faces. We were embraced and advised that this would be our new vocation and now a part of a vital routine. "Paul," he was told, "you must watch your water intake, suck on lemon pits and chopped ice to quench your thirst, keep your potassium low, and never give up because you *can* live!" Tales of individuals on dialysis for many years abound. We stayed in the waiting room while Paul was connected to his new lifeline. In time, we would come to know and understand the philosophical importance of this new passage in our lives. The symbolism of this "connection" was profound. As he integrated the experience of dialysis into his life, Paul reflected on his past and questioned what the future would bring. Twelve hours each week were to be dedicated to this forced commitment, and everyone had a story and something poignant to impart to each other while in treatment. These purposeful relationships began as he was welcomed into the dialysis family by persons young and old, diverse in ethnicity, income, and perspectives, and meant to be connected to each other. It also became an opportunity for our family—an unforeseen time to redefine relationships and reflect on and share stories in and about the waiting room. Quickly we all understood that, truly, the best gift we can give to each other is this *time*.

Rocky's Fight/Plight

> We choose our joys and sorrows long before we experience them.
>
> —Kahlil Gibran

It was another Saturday night, and the cast entered the waiting room. Sarah, a delightful elderly person who had become reliant on outside transportation (as many patients have); Sam, another patient, just returning from being hospitalized; and Rocky, entered stage left and the performance began. Everyone shared their experiences of the week and current health situations—bouts of diabetes, arthritis, and fluid intake levels—the many challenges they had come to know and navigate daily. Rocky, a man in his mid-fifties and, from stories told, a very successful entrepreneur in the technology area, was also totally reliant on outside transportation and always had a tale to tell. He was called Rocky at his request. Self-declared and all alone, each week Rocky voiced his wish for a home and someone to love. In the absence of such, his dog served as his companion, and it was getting increasingly difficult for Rocky to care for him. Rocky was a severe diabetic who had experienced many complications with sores, back problems, and the like. He consistently vied for nurturance and attention, and his care of himself was questionable. If he could find a kind ear, his stories would begin—Were they the whole truth? No one knew. He claimed that he was without food and care as such—the tales went on and on, and the kind ear listened intently in the waiting room.

All of us need a place to be, to contribute, to belong, and to be loved. Rocky was in search of all that in this special place. It was this quiet Saturday night that Rocky entered carrying with him a bag filled with foods toxic to his diabetes. Rumor had it that he convinced his ambulette drivers to take him to the neighborhood take-out places on his way to the center in exchange for a free meal.

He was connected to the dialysis machine, and time passed. To compensate for his food intake, Rocky took out a syringe and got ready to inject insulin. Once the charge nurse witnessed this action, she immediately urged him to put down the syringe, as dialysis cleanses the body of sugar, and insulin could overmedicate him. A physical altercation ensued, for Rocky wanted it *his* way even though it was not in *his* best interest. As we sat in the waiting room taking in the events of this evening's antics, we became privy to Rocky's personal history.

To us, he portrayed someone who felt that life had little value and that he was being cheated out of his share. Everyone has a legacy and history, and Rocky longed for his to be told. What was supposed to be the story of a young, successful man with a bright future and promise became the complete opposite. He was now committed to a life of solitude and dependent on a walker and a dialysis machine. He was someone who subtly reminded us of the pain of loneliness, appreciation of family, and community connection. Truly, his only link appeared to be new and gentle souls who would listen intently to his story for the first time. His longing for happiness was apparent, and his sense of purpose and survival was severely threatened by his depression, yet he carried on. We soon came to know that one of Rocky's most gratifying experiences in his lonely life was his sense of independence that one time per year when, at Christmastime, he would walk around the store, trying to select the perfect gift for each family member on his limited list. This sense of freedom and belonging allowed Rocky that special feeling of love and family ties, at least for the moment.

As the rest of the year progressed, Rocky developed sores and infections common to poorly maintained diabetes, which went well beyond medical care to control. He was forced to endure a double amputation of his legs, leaving Rocky more dependent and isolated. Rocky had since left this world, but his spirit now soars with the freedom and finesse that his body and mind would not allow him on earth!

Moving In Together

> Once you make a decision, the universe conspires
> to make it happen.
>
> —Ralph Waldo Emerson

Another member of our dialysis family, Steve, was a gentle soul, also stricken by diabetes, visual impairment, and a failed kidney transplant. With his strong will and perseverance, he lay in wait for another compatible kidney. On any given night, one could constantly find him in the waiting room, sharing kind words of encouragement to fellow patients while displaying a genuine interest in the welfare of his comrades. He was truly a resilient man despite the challenges he faced from the past and the uncertainty of his future. His compromised health was pitted against a courageous soul in search of love, connection, and contribution; his chance, and his choice. One of the brightest moments he shared with us in the waiting room was his declaration of love and commitment to his love, a true soul mate. She now shared our space as she anticipated his return to the waiting room.

Drivers' Tales

> Over every mountain, there is a path, although it
> may not be seen from the valley.
>
> —James Rogers

Transportation is a critical part of the dialysis equation, and many drivers join in sharing their parables in the waiting room, contributing to the dialogue and social network. They, too, become connected and convey their respective challenges, triumphs, and dreams.

Joy, a very compassionate and dedicated mother of one, was a dialysis transporter who lost her husband when her son was very young. Her sensitivity to the pain of those she transported gave each one of them a sense of comfort during this difficult time in their lives. In the waiting room, she shared her pride in her son readily and her commitment to his well-being and happiness. The only gift she was unable to give her son was the gift of time, as she was the sole breadwinner of her little family.

John was another frequent visitor to the waiting room, who drove as a second job to support his six children. He was quite a traditional man and father, constantly worrying about their welfare, the temptations of modern-day society, and the strength of his children to remain resilient and productive in a chaotic world. His wish was to purchase a home for them, and each week, he would arrive with a status report—interest rates were going down and homes were now more affordable. This had been a several-year journey for him until, finally, he had found something that he could afford and that would accommodate his family comfortably within a safe neighborhood. He was content in achieving this milestone and looked forward to embedding his roots. For him, his children were always his legacy, his definition, and something he pridefully boasted about in the waiting room.

For the Love of a Grandfather

> What greater thing is there for human souls than
> to feel that they are joined for life—to be with
> each other in silent, unspeakable memories?
>
> —George Eliot

Meet Steven, a fourteen-year-old who could always be found with a sketch pad in hand each week, passing the time in the waiting room while waiting for his grandfather to finish his dialysis treatment. His grandfather was a wonderful role model to him, unconditionally dedicated to his education and welfare. Steven was a self-proclaimed artist who wanted to pursue a career in graphic design. His creativity and imagination were only surpassed by his uncanny sensitivity to others who surrounded him. He was viewed by all as an old soul, and while in the waiting room, he made his contribution, helping patients who were alone, sharing a smile, reporting on his efforts at school, and articulating his dreams. Each night, he would leave, backpack in one hand and the other gently supporting his grandfather, only to be seen again next week when he returned once again to the waiting room.

Sam's Place

The only true gift is a portion of yourself.

—Ralph Waldo Emerson

Meet Sam, an attractive senior citizen who always entered the waiting room with greetings and a smile. His wife, Joan, was confined to a wheelchair and entered the center with much trepidation. Sam and Joan lived a very full and enriched life. Their home was always seen as the center of their social network. As Joan's health began to deteriorate and her kidney values diminished, she was also introduced to the dialysis machine.

Sam was a loving and dedicated husband, who faithfully sat by her side throughout her treatment, consoling, appealing to, and calming her spirit. Joan had never embraced this reality and continued to fight and resent it for all she was worth. They both entered this waiting room hoping for an equitable compromise. Being a caretaker creates a tremendous amount of stress and strain on one's mind, heart, and spirit. Sam's health had steadily declined, and his children now faithfully endured the task of accompanying *him* into the waiting room.

My Son

> Children will not remember you for the material
> things you provided, but for the feeling that you
> cherished them.
>
> —Richard L. Evans

It was another relatively quiet evening on the late shift, and the unit was just about to finish up for the night. Paul waited anxiously for the fourth hour to end. With thirty minutes left, a gentleman gingerly wheeled himself toward him. Reportedly, he was a new patient from a local nursing home, alone and with little to say, quite introspective. Looking at the back of this gentleman's head, one would think it was Paul's brother, Anthony, who departed almost five years earlier.

The gentleman stopped and, with a fixed look of tears in his eyes and with a weakened voice, proclaimed, "I held you in my arms, my son." Paul's eyes welled up, and his heart was immediately filled. He acknowledged this man without disrupting the illusion. For the moment, this gentleman was connected to his past and was fulfilled.

The old man left with elation, believing that his son had come back to him in the waiting room. He was not seen or heard from again!

John's Tale

> Life is what happens to you while you're busy
> making other plans.
>
> —John Lennon

John was just about forty years of age and came to dialysis with his head held high, full of life and living. He faithfully brought his laptop, cell phone, and books to maximize his time, maintain his spirit, and affirm that life was worth living. Each night, he greeted his comrades with a gesture of support, sincere interest, and a broad and encompassing smile.

John never anticipated the need for dialysis, nor might it have been his predetermined destiny. His story was quite different and very powerful. John went to the doctor, not feeling well. Blood tests were repeatedly taken, and he was sent on his way with the illusion that all was clear. Subsequently, he fell ill to flu-like symptoms and eventually went to the hospital, where they discovered that he was in renal failure with less than two hours to live.

Over the last several years, he had courageously entered the waiting room, having experienced much loss in his family life. He found solace in his brother, extended family, and committed friends as he eagerly pursued a kidney transplant. For John, he had accepted this new reality in his life and continued to find purpose and meaning in the path that lay ahead.

Meet Mrs. Jones

> Old age, believe me, is a good and pleasant thing.
> Indeed, you are gently shouldered off the stage,
> but then you are given such a comfortable front
> stall as spectator.
>
> —Confucius

Mrs. Jones was a gentle old soul, eager to converse and receptive to a smile and kind gesture. She lived with her husband and gradually deteriorated to a residence at an area nursing home. Her main ambition was to return home, those familiar surroundings that gave her purpose and stability and told her story.

Her husband faithfully visited her at the nursing home each day and consistently accompanied her into the waiting room as part of his daily regimen. Although illness set in and she lost part of her limbs, what always remained constant in her heart was a vision that she kept of "going home."

As her dialysis went late into the evening, oftentimes she would be found alone in the waiting room, anxiously anticipating her ambulette and someone to remain with her. Many evenings, we did so and were blessed with the glow of her smile and the warmth of her heart. Then, one evening, there was an uneasy stillness in the waiting room. It was late, and Mrs. Jones had not arrived. It was then that we came to realize that she had been granted her wish and "went home." Mrs. Jones, you are missed, and our lives have been enriched by the many gifts you have bestowed upon us.

Transitioning into the Human Connection

> My satisfaction comes from my commitment to advancing a better world.
>
> —Faye Wattleton

Each week, patients shared time, stories, and perceptions and the staff, one big extended family. These connections were no accident. Tony left and came back—as he truly had cultivated relationships that were difficult to let go. Sarah's family resided in Africa with her husband, and each week she recounted the events of their children's lives. Janice was a single mom working hard to be a responsible parent. Each one brought an extraordinary commitment to the waiting room, as they left their indelible marks on the many patients and their families they encountered and truly embraced.

Where Are They All Going?

> The ultimate measure of a man is not where he stands in moments of comfort and convenience, but where he stands at times of challenge and controversy.
>
> —Martin Luther King Jr.

Another week passes, and Paul's nausea makes him very uncomfortable. This was the one week of the month concurrently dedicated to chemotherapy. His spirit diminished, as his body and mind were wearing. He wondered, *How much longer can this go on? What is this doing to my family who have already struggled with my life's challenges and behavior through the years?* Dialysis was something that his body could not do without, although it stretched the ability of the mind and body to endure. Five patients remained and the hour was late. All was quiet when bells and alarms interrupt the silence—blood pressures were low and sequentially four patients either pass out or are on the verge. Emergency procedures were put into place and ambulances were called to transport each patient to the hospital alone. Paul remained on his dialysis machine, relieved that this time, it was not his crisis to bear.

Learning the Ropes

> By learning, you will teach. By teaching, you will learn.
>
> —Latin Proverb

Knowledge is truly *power*. It was summertime and a slow Thursday night. Paul entered the waiting room and graciously extended greetings to those few in his path. As always, he sat quietly as he was connected to the dialysis machine. To his surprise, upon entry, the needle nicked an artery, and the arm immediately began to swell. Filled with anxiety, he was comforted by staff and told that this was not an uncommon occurrence. Staff members patiently administered ice and took this time to educate him about the evolution of dialysis. Reference was made to the chronology of events that became the protocols of dialysis as we know it today. This technology grew from being available on a limited basis to help the lives of thousands of people throughout the world today.

All of us were truly educated about the dialysis experience and how fortunate we were to have this readily available. Paul was not a candidate for a kidney transplant because of his myelodysplastic syndrome (MDS). The transplant protocol at that time only allowed individuals that were cancer-free for five years. For candidates awaiting a kidney and those with anticipated extended dialysis, they will remain in the waiting room.

Fast-Forward to the End or Beginning?

We live, not as we wish to, but as we can.

—Mencius

It was now December 1, 2007, and another session at dialysis. As we gathered for the evening, the waiting room was full and the dialogue varied. Paul arrived in much pain down the leg and back and was barely able to sit through his four-hour treatment. Everyone attributed this pain to a pinched nerve and did what they could to make him comfortable and the pain tolerable. However, despite their efforts, the pain persisted, and he went home hoping that the next day would bring relief.

Sunday brought a terrific storm—hail, snow, rain, and sleet— car accidents abounded. At midday, all of us received a call. Paul's left leg was still in pain and had turned colors. It was clear that the blood was not flowing into it, and immediate assistance was necessary to save it. Paul and Dorothy called the surgeon (who had previously done the bypass surgery on his leg) to find that he was on vacation. The covering doctor recommended that he immediately go to the emergency room for treatment. Upon arrival, Paul and Dorothy were greeted by Dr. J, who advised them that the bypass was no longer functioning, and the leg was dying from lack of nourishment. It was unknown without testing exactly what could be done—where the blockage was—and the unspoken was present in everyone's mind… "Could the leg be saved?"

Yet another detour on this voyage, another unknown, and once again, we drew upon our belief and the competency of the surgeon to bring life back to his leg and allow him the freedom to walk again. In this darkest moment, all of us pondered the potential outcome silently. What would it mean for him to now lose mobility? It was unspoken freedom and a critical time, for without it, a dependence would be created that Paul's ego could not and would not endure.

We prayed, asked questions, and went through the motions. The testing was completed over the next few days and confirmed that the arteries below the initial bypass had closed down and those above it narrowed. Surgery was not the only hope! Days passed before he was able to withstand the procedure. The myelodysplastic syndrome (MDS) that had compromised his blood also provided extreme risk to this type of surgery and potential intensive bleeding, in and of itself, could have killed him. So with each day, the leg darkened, and the anxiety elevated. With each day, new prayers were put forth, as it now appeared that we needed a miracle.

It was now Thursday, December 6, and Dr. M, (the surgeon who had completed the initial bypass) returned. Paul was now ready for the surgery. Our thoughts, questions, concerns, and fears wandered through our minds as hours passed. The surgery was predicted to be one and one-half hours in duration. With the stakes so high, this seemed to be an eternity in the waiting room. The tension mounted as the silence remained and the pacing began. It was a cold, damp evening, and the family was huddled in the corner together in relative stillness. Each one of us was pondering the outcome, awaiting the verdict and knowing full well that this might be another defining moment. Dr. M entered the waiting room in his scrubs, perspiration on his brow. The operation was complicated, but the blood was finally flowing, the leg had life, and Paul, another chance. We now entered a critical twenty-four-hour period of avoiding infection to assure the bypass was working and that the operation was successful.

Paul entered recovery, still partially under anesthesia but seemingly exuberant to realize that he would have another opportunity. He proclaimed his love for all and admitted the fear of the unspoken but was relieved that he would not face it at this particular moment in time. The next day, he entered the intensive care unit and was greeted with intravenous drugs, monitors, painkillers, and medical staff. His condition, fortunately, remained stable. He passively endured dialysis and two blood transfusions and was willing to do *anything* just to attain the freedom to walk again. Though the pain-killers alleviated the discomfort, his mind continued to integrate this experience, becoming increasingly introspective, greeting his family and friends with few words and blank stares. The next day, he was moved to the surgical unit and placed near the nursing station for maximum monitoring.

That evening, the leg swelled, darkened in color, and once again, he was in great pain. Morphine was administered, and he retreated into a deep sleep. Dr. M was called, and a hospital intern arrived. Thankfully, this was an anticipated outcome, as the leg had not gotten the required nourishment over some time. His healing, however, was going as well as they expected. To draw an analogy, sometimes when we pass through life with blinders on and cannot or will not take in our realities, it can be painful when we do. So too Paul's leg, absent of blood and nourishment, experienced pain before the process of healing.

Dorothy faithfully remained at his side every moment. She combated her exhaustion with prayer and a desire to return Paul to his physical status before this grueling event. We adjourned to the waiting room once again to greet this outcome with the courage that a bonded family amasses.

Paul's room was switched, and it was here that he was about to encounter yet another earth angel to make the road he was traveling more tolerable. Meet Gabby, a ninety-one-year-old man with the spirit and zest of a child. He had been admitted to the hospital and recently had surgery for some type of gastrointestinal blockage. He self-reported from the "home." His wife had been admitted to the nursing home several years back as her health complications extended well beyond Gabby's ability to care for her. As a result of his loneliness and not wanting to continually "stare at the walls and the memories," he voluntarily admitted himself as well. It was not an accident that Gabby shared this room and moment in Paul's life. Quick with a joke, he painted the room with joy and laughter. When Paul had his less than lucid moments, he watched out for him—

quickly notifying the nurse when he felt that Paul's health status was changing or compromised.

In a short time, Gabby's stated role was clear. As Paul continued to heal, he spent hours in a chair beside Gabby, exchanging stories, memories, history, and encouragement. Paul was healing and enlightened by his spirit and warmth. Throughout our lives, we are enriched by human connections well beyond our family—unlikely strangers perhaps, and Gabby was a deliberate addition to this chapter…no accident. As family and friends continued to visit Paul, they extended themselves to Gabby, and he was outwardly fulfilled. He provided daily reports, oral history, and laughter and felt a strong purpose. The day he was discharged, Paul was markedly better, and Gabby's purpose was achieved. He and Paul were both fulfilled and on the mend.

With so many complications and the introduction of major surgery, the body's balance was disrupted. That evening, a kind middle-aged nurse named Debbie greeted us. She was extremely empathetic and reassuring. In time, she shared her story. In caring for her sick husband, she discovered *her* vocation/calling. Then, she persistently completed her education and vowed that her competence would always be matched by her proclaimed compassion for patients, and it certainly was! As the evening progressed, perspiration was visible on Paul's brow, and he became quite disoriented. His sugar was bottoming out as his blood pressure dropped. The family stayed to assure that the necessary care was available and only left when they knew that Debbie would watch over him and call at intervals to assure his stability.

Days passed, and it was now time for Paul to return home. Exhausted, the entire family greeted this day with joy and optimism that Paul's independence and freedom would be maintained. With over one hundred staples in his leg, he gingerly arrived home to begin the long recuperation as a further enriched human being. He was confined to a wheelchair for a while, but the outlook was good.

That Saturday, he returned to his dialysis family, fully tooled to share these experiences and relieved that the outcome was favorable. We returned to the waiting room with renewed strength in having yet another opportunity. As we traveled this ebb and flow in life, many experiences provided balance. One of the things we learned to do was to open our hearts and minds to utilize these experiences.

It was now January 2008 and the beginning of a new year. Paul had undergone twenty-seven rounds of chemotherapy (according to his doctor, this was the longest that anyone had been successfully maintained on this chemo protocol at the time), and on dialysis for fifteen months and holding. Paul's leg was mending, and his spirits continued to wander. Relieved that the surgery was successful, he moved closer to regaining his independence, relinquishing the wheelchair, and returning to the garage for daily visits with his neighborhood family.

The Garage Club was quite a unique bunch. Paul was known as the ringleader, with John and Nick as devoted members. Each day, they gathered to share their perceptions of the world, settle the neighborhood affairs, and support each other. This was a mainstay of Paul's day when he wasn't busily going to doctors, dialysis, or chemotherapy. It was in this garage that his neighborhood comrades surrounded him with love and provided a safe place for him to be, to contribute, and to belong. We have always been eternally grateful for this bond.

Paul also relied on Dorothy's strength and sanguinity. Dorothy refueled her spirit and creativity through reading, beadwork, crossword puzzles with members of her neighborhood and St. Thomas Church, consistently surrounded by their love, encouragement, and support. She greeted each day with renewed optimism and faith, as these were her strongest assets to cope with her frequent visits to the waiting room. Dorothy was, however, getting weary. As she diligently accompanied Paul to each visit, tracked his progress, changed his bandages, and helped mend his spirit, she was visibly tired and drained. Her world continued to revolve around his health, and her moods were gauged by his progress. Though she had much life left in her, she had little energy, time, or opportunity for any recreation or social life as she continued to face each new challenge that came their way.

The Caretaker

You need to commit, and once you make it, then life will give you some answers

—Les Brown

Just a few thoughts about the role of caretaker. It takes a tremendous amount of selflessness to play this role. Your world revolves around the person you are caring for, your life is on hold, and at times, you are overwhelmed with feelings of hopelessness. "Am I doing the right thing, asking the correct questions? Did I miss anything? Where will this road ultimately take us? Should I be more aggressive or less? Should we seek another medical opinion?" So much of the caretaker's life becomes defined by this important role embedded in the love of and the connection to another human being. Truly, not everyone has someone in his or her life willing to make this sacrifice, with no regrets. Paul was extremely fortunate, and he truly understood that!

In researching this role a bit further, we happened upon an article from the National Family Caregivers Association www.thefamily-caregiver.org which we felt was worth sharing. It certainly resonated with us. It goes like this.

MESSAGES TO LIVE BY…

We all have lessons to learn throughout our lifetimes. Life evolves and sometimes our journey takes us through turbulent waters and other times the waters remain still. These journeys become a part of us and make us who we are. We are here to learn from one another and through these lessons, we can heal our relationships and sometimes ourselves.

Becoming a family caregiver for someone you love is one of those heart-wrenching and at times enlightening life lessons. Your role as a family caregiver can happen abruptly or creep in slowly unnoticed until one day you realize you are caring more for someone else than you are for yourself.

You find yourself beginning to struggle with the day-to-day demands and somewhere along the way you realize you have lost your identity and have allowed the caregiving role to define who you are. Your new role as a family caregiver can become as frightening as the initial diagnosis. **The journey can be difficult when traveled alone; however, you do not and should not have to travel the road alone.**

Dorothy and Paul's relationship exemplified yin and yang. Where one ended, the other began. They were able to finish each other's sentences and anticipated each other's responses. Oftentimes, they traveled the road to medical appointments without uttering a word, and it was fine, as they were *still* together, finding peace in each other's silence.

In the waiting room, we embraced lessons learned with a humble heart and open mind—constantly wondering where all of this would be going. What was the meaning and our intended purpose in the waiting room? Diverse emotions were experienced that were foreign to the normalcy of life as we knew it. We felt pain, anger, hope, and confusion. It became a consistent roller coaster of emotions and, at times, difficult to manage. Each time the telephone rang, or a blood test was taken, a doctor called, or a new pain emerged, we just didn't know where the day would end. This was truly our place at the moment, in this waiting room, constantly praying that tomorrow would bring some answers and relief!

And the Gates of Heaven Opened to Welcome Home an Angel

An individual has not started living until he can rise above the narrow confines of his individualistic concerns to the broader concerns of all humanity.

—Martin Luther King Jr.

Because I could not stop for death, it kindly stopped for me.

—Emily Dickenson

Every day, in the world around us, real-life angels are doing the things they do…and bringing more smiles to the rest of us. They build bridges instead of walls. They don't play hide-and-seek with the truth, and they don't have hidden agendas. They tend to be the only ones who understand what you're going through. If they sense that you're hurting, they do whatever they can to help. These earth angels are individuals who walk among us with the intended purpose of showing us the way—positive role models. They are quite extraordinary in that their influence is great and their perception of themselves reserved.

Meet Ann, a very dear friend of the family who was an integral part in coping with the many trials and tribulations brought on by Paul's illness. She had known our family for over twenty years, joined in many of our family holidays and celebrations, and shepherded us through many challenges. Her connection to our family was a true gift and her lessons profound! She was truly *our* earth angel.

Ann's roots were in Virginia. Her love of the Blue Ridge Mountains, lakes, and countryside was unsurpassed! This was her home and always remained so in her heart. Her core family was there—"brother" Bob and his wife, Chris; niece Kimberly and her husband, Paul, and two children, Will and Delia! They provided her with abundant love, enriching experiences, and a strong foundation for her investment in human services.

Her life's mission was her work in New York, and there she cultivated her northern "family in service." These were individuals and extended family members with whom she shared many life journeys—those who eventually help *her* transition "home." It was not uncommon to find Ann in the waiting room nurturing, cajoling, encouraging, and lending her strength. She introduced us to many firsts—our first opera, art, music, current affairs, diverse perspectives, southern lifestyle, and unreserved kindness. Ann always made people feel so special when she was with them. She was a very accomplished but humble soul who would always lend reason to chaos, and wisdom to obscurity.

She was truly an extended family member and was loved by all! It was no accident that she came into our lives when she did, enriching us with her lessons. For Paul, she represented his conscience. While he did not agree with her *all* the time, he certainly listened to her wisdom and was in awe of her gentle spirit, many accomplishments, and the love shared with those whose lives she so genuinely touched. He took heart from her character, optimism, and great sense of hope.

Ann was a champion advocate for children, as her career was dedicated to fighting for the most vulnerable, assuring their voice and place in the community was heard. After thirty-five years of an illustrious career, she retired a true living legacy. In April 1998, she underwent surgery to remove a lump that, at first, was interpreted as benign. To our horror, it was discovered that she had breast cancer, a sentence that would forever test her fortitude and will as a *true* survivor! The cancer was so advanced that during Memorial Day weekend that year, she underwent a full mastectomy. Thereafter, she continued her life's work—promoting youth, family, and community development—with an extended hand to all who needed the touch of her love, faith, patience, and competence.

She mentored those who had recently been diagnosed with breast cancer and served as an exemplar to all! In 2001, there was a recurrence at the mastectomy scar site, which was quickly removed and immediately followed by daily radiation. In 2005, she had a serious car accident that required hospitalization for an extended period. From the trauma unit to the cardiac floor, she persevered with renewed commitment and determination, as in her heart she knew that she had more to do in this life. Later that year, after having experienced prolonged lower back pain and elevated cancer markers, she gallantly returned to her oncologist only to find that the breast cancer had unfortunately metastasized. Once again, Ann was forced to endure chemotherapy, and she audaciously survived without questioning why. Less than one year later, the markers were again elevated, and the completed scans indicated that the breast cancer had now spread throughout her bones, and treatment continued. Each week, Ann greeted Thursday's sunrise on the Long Island Expressway to Manhattan and returned home weary and tired, yet persistent with faith. Life continued.

Paul witnessed her ordeal as it unfolded, and he took heart from her example. He used to always reflect, "Look at what she has had to endure…I can get through this…" Fast-forward to Easter, March 2008. After dinner that evening, it was clear that Ann was not feeling well, as she sat silently with the pain of breast cancer and the latest sinus infection. She was taken to the hospital, confused and afraid but never alone. The priority: find the cause of the infection and confusion. Hours turned to days, and Ann began experiencing seizure activity. The doctors suspected that cancer had spread to her brain. Their first order of business was to control the infection and stabilize the seizures. An MRI was therefore scheduled immediately, hoping that it would supply them with the critical piece of the puzzle in Ann's diagnosis and treatment plan.

As time passed, Ann lost consciousness, but her ears, heart, and spirit remained open to kind words, lots of prayers, and the power of the loving touch that her "family in service" and friends provided. The MRI, unfortunately, was not able to yield any definitive answers, so it was decided that the antibiotic treatment would continue, and a lumbar puncture test was to be administered.

Ann remained in a comatose state, only waking briefly and just enough to let us know that she chose to continue this fight and required all of us to join her! Her eyes opened for that moment, and a word was uttered, keeping hope alive. It was now ten days later in the waiting room, and the suspicion remained that cancer had spread to the brain. Private care assistants were made available twenty-four seven to join the team of those who cared—coaching, encouraging, and giving their personal best to a woman, a legacy, who always did the same for everyone. It was now her time to receive.

Another day passed, anxiously awaiting the results of the pathology report. Anxiety filled the air as we were preparing to take the next critical step to keep Ann alive. These times, marked by sheer exhaustion, were fueled by a deep commitment and responsibility to battle *with* and for her. Her infrequent words were our gift—her momentary smile ignited our energy as we continued toward an unknown destination. We gave her our best, as she now required no less and had given no less to any and all. A deluge of memories and images of her gentle spirit and selflessness entered our hearts. As we reflected on this time, this moment, we also thought of the unique roles she had played in each of our lives, encouraging our inherent abilities while challenging us to reach for new heights and make *our* mark.

One of our most profound images thinking of Ann would be that of her cultivating her garden, tenderly creating a place for each plant to be and expand, nourishing the roots and enriching its growth. This was much the same way that she conducted her life. She had enriched all of us like a shepherd, calmly guiding her flock to greener pastures—always redirecting, challenging, and keeping us of one accord. As one of her friends, Dr. Barbara Thompson, so eloquently stated:

The beauty and value of Ann's Garden was
a testament to her hard work and passion for life.

It is peaceful in her garden where you are surrounded by lush greenery, cool moist soil, and colorful explosions of flowers. The scent of the flowers and the soil is carried on the breeze that whispers through the garden. When you walk around, looking at the plants and the flowers, you are amazed to think that someone grew them from seeds and starters…and that definitive care and work brought this entire explosion of color into the world. Ann, we are all your garden… Each of us is a flower with unique character… color and form.

Two weeks almost passed, and Ann went deeper into unconsciousness but was still aware we were surrounding her. She continued offering glimpses of hope as she struggled to open one eye, nod, speak, or firmly hold our hands. She knew that she was loved in the same way that she had loved throughout her lifetime. Many of us felt that she was in a partial state of renewal—the past, the present, and the future. We wondered if we were about to face the moment when her spirit would soar and know that her fate was now well beyond the competence of doctors and *our* will!

Twelve days later, we returned home. The lumbar puncture results had been compromised and must be completed again. With this outcome once again deferred, we returned to the waiting room. This very day, to our joy, Ann opened both of her eyes, remaining with us for some time, sharing a smile, acknowledging a picture, responding to the love that filled the room. Her determination remained while she continued to give us strength as we gave her courage. It was now thirteen days later, and we awoke to the sunshine of a placid spring morning, only tempered by the realities of this journey.

We all got lost in our thoughts, recalling and celebrating the moments we'd shared and still desperately searching for an answer. As we sat and pondered, we awaited a sign, anything that would forecast light on the next turn in the road. As we looked up at the sky, two finches flew within one foot of our eyes, and we remained hopeful. Ann so loved the birds and took great responsibility and joy in their nourishment. Was this a sign? As the wind of their wings almost touched our brows, it renewed our strength to go on and face the challenges that lay ahead. Seventeen long days had now passed and plans for hospice care had been initiated. Two months turned into two weeks, and at this moment, we faced two days or less! It now became her plan and the will of God. Her life-giving tubes were removed, all tests ceased, the morphine drip was administered, and we waited in anticipation for this angel to attain her wings and soar. We now had to let her go—to a new life and the voyage that would reunite her with loved ones who had gone before, perched in a place where she would forever touch our lives.

Her spirit was in our hearts as she readied for this journey. She was finally at peace, knowing that her work here was complete. Throughout this time, she continued to teach us the value of the dash between our birth and passing. These were truly her defining moments, surrounded by the love that she had cultivated and treated with the respect and dignity she so valued in life. She left behind a legacy and a foundation that each of us could draw from in our darkest moments and a motivation to pay it forward to those who needed a voice, a hand that needed to be grasped, or a heart to be fulfilled. She had mattered, and our world, minds, and spirits knew that we had been touched by an angel.

In the final days, some of us arrived at the hospital early to capture as many moments as possible, sharing a turn reflecting with her on our times together with much gratitude. She was peaceful now, possessing a glow that made us know that the gates of heaven were now preparing for her arrival. As each of us exited, we knew full well in our hearts that this could well be the last time. On April 18, 2008, our Ann attained her wings at 7:40 a.m. while the sun was shining and the birds were calling her name. She went "home."

As we celebrated the life and legacy of Ann, we came to realize the value of the lessons learned from her final journey in this waiting room and the irony (or not) of all of us assuming her role as a "voice" for *her* as she passed through. These lessons centered on dignity and respect, humility and character. In one of the many tributes that paid homage to her life and example, the following passage was read:

> Ann, you truly have had a heart big enough to embrace all of us. Your spirit, character, kindness, and love have enriched our families with memories we will each hold for the rest of our lives.
>
> We join many others as your extended family in deep sorrow and great celebration of you, a phenomenal woman who had done so much for so many.
>
> You have taught us by example, encouraged and supported us—providing poignant life lessons that will remain in our hearts, always!
>
> You are truly an angel who we are proud to include in our families' lives and eternally grateful for the many gifts you have given to us, our children, and countless others. As your spirit soars with the angels in Heaven, always know that we are all better people because of you and you have, truly, made a difference!
>
> She has earned her wings now, and her spirit and lessons will be in our hearts forever; a voice for youth, a conscience for all! As the gates of Heaven open to embrace you, rest in peace knowing that your life's work here is now done. God Bless You!

The Aftermath

> Death, be not the dark cloud hovering over my aspirations; be to me a passive friend, guiding me through the darkest realm of an undiscovered world;

Stand still to those who would value the generosity of thy hand, and come quickly to those who live no longer. Be there in the still of the night, not the cause of that great darkness; You are to us part of the mysterious workmanship of our universe that we seek to understand; Grant us patience for we have yet to realize the vitality in our living world.

—AMZ

Days flowed into weeks, and we were about to mark the two-month anniversary. The mourning process evolved from disbelief to a deep sense of loss. She was forever gone, and we continued to draw on the memories, photos, and teachings she had given as we contemplated this concept of *forever*.

As we exited this chapter in the waiting room and began to heal, we reflected on this journey and will do so for a very long time to come. We will always know and remain in the tranquility of *her* garden.

Through this experience and in helping her transition to the "other side," she continued to teach us. People were awakened to each other; new relationships were cultivated and old ones renewed. It seemed that when moments like this came into our lives, they served as an opportunity to take off the blinders, put the guard down, and embrace each other in different ways—the common denominator—sharing this prolific experience in the waiting room.

Reconciliation

The Darkness Before the Dawn

The Dash:

I read of a man who stood to speak at the funeral of his friend. He referred to the dates on his tombstone from the beginning...to the end. He noted that first comes the date of his birth and spoke of the second with tears when said that what mattered most of all was the dash between those years. The dash represents all the time that he spent alive on earth. And now only those who loved him know what that little line is worth. For it matters not, how much we own; the cars, the house, the cash. What matters is how we live and love and how we spend our dash. So, think about this long and hard, are there things you'd like to change? For you never know how much time is left. (You could be at 'dash mid-range'). If we could just slow down enough to consider what's true and what's real, and always try to understand the way other people feel. And...be less quick to anger, and show appreciation more and love the people in our lives as we'd never loved before. If we treat each other with respect, and more often wear a smile, remembering that this special dash might only last a little while. So, when

your eulogy is being read with your life's actions
to rehash…would you be pleased with the things
they have to say about how you spent your dash?
(Source Unknown)

It was now June 19, 2008, close to the summer solstice. Solstices occur twice a year. The name is derived from the Latin *sol* (sun) and *sistere* (to stand still). At the solstices, the sun stands still in declination; that is, its apparent movement north or south comes to a standstill. This term, from a broader perspective, is referred to as the date that such a passage occurs. In essence, it is the separation of seasons—like life and…beyond? Incidentally (or not), June 19 was the anniversary of Paul's sister, Janet's passing.

We awaken to a new journey. Paul was now put on another type of chemotherapy as the first had outlasted its usefulness. Despite the 20 percent chance of this chemotherapy being effective, we remained hopeful that quality of life could be somewhat sustained. The periods of nausea, however, became the constant, causing Paul extreme fatigue and weakness; but by the grace of God, he was surviving. During this time, he confided to his Garage Club that his time may be short, and he did not want to leave Dottie like this. Life's reflections started meshing together as he contemplated all of his yesterdays, holding on to each moment of the present and pondering the future. He was truly in a dilemma and not ready to let go, not yet!

On Father's Day (2008), Paul stayed awake most of the day, which was quite unusual due to the advanced state of his illness. His children, grandchildren, and caring neighbors fulfilled him as his ears embraced the sounds of their laughter and his eyes beheld his legacy and the love and beauty of this day and celebration. As the week progressed, his fatigue increased, the blank stares continued, and he became further weakened and introspective. He arose this Thursday, June 19, to prepare for his almost daily ritual of medical visits. As he gingerly tried to move about, he came to realize that he could not stand, was dazed, and needed immediate assistance. He had come upon another crisis, which necessitated a return to the emergency room.

With great trepidation, we found ourselves once again in the waiting room too. Knowing that his new chemotherapy might not be working, we were faced with the realization that his time may be short. We continued to pray for a miracle, for that would be the only thing that would keep Paul with us. Again, it was time to stand together and prepare for the next step, perhaps the final chapter. Symbolically, many of us interpreted his blank stares as the beginning of *his* renewal process, looking at his life, integrating the joy of family, and contemplating his future in the waiting room. His health was visibly failing, and the doctor and ambulance were called so Paul could be taken back to the hospital once again.

His tests were completed, the transfusions began, and Paul was renewed for this moment with the hope of soon returning to his loving home. With a new weekend arriving, Paul suffered another blood level drop, requiring yet another transfusion. At this point in Paul's life, it was now determined that he was transfusion dependent. His nausea continued, and all efforts were being made to understand this crisis and try to return him to a prior quality of life.

It was now Monday, June 23, 2008, and we stood strong as a family in hope that we would soon come to know and understand Paul's destabilized state. He entered deeper and deeper into himself and inwardly held onto the lifetime of love that had never left him. As his status steadily declined, invasive testing was nixed, and the family braced for uncharted waters. As the day progressed, Paul's left leg transformed in color, the blood supply was decreased substantially, and he was in a severely compromised state. We entered this waiting room with few options, tempered hope, and an abundance of reminiscences. All of Paul's doctors convened to assess his crisis, only to find themselves in a quandary.

Efforts to surgically repair his leg could take his life, and the absence of such action could cause infection with the same outcome. His white blood count was dangerously low, and his strength of mind was diminished as he continued *this* fight for his life. A ray of hope illuminated when the doctors chose to administer heparin to salvage the minimal circulation that remained in Paul's leg and an antibiotic regimen to keep the infection at bay. While we waited for the treatment to commence and Paul silently lay in retreat, each one of us succumbed to our own waiting room, contemplating this potential transformation of our lives (and his), forever.

Our psyche remained raw from Ann's passing less than two months prior, and our hearts were not yet poised for another great loss. Before us lay a "superman" with the stature and hands big enough to subsume ours, always making us feel so safe. As we held his hand now, at this particular moment, we poignantly recalled our childhood—walking with him, our hands lost in his grip. We were afraid to take this walk unaccompanied by his strength, knowing that this journey would ultimately have to be done alone.

It was now Tuesday, June 24, 2008, and our eldest sibling, Donna, was called back to New York, anticipating Paul's fragile condition. Donna's arrival galvanized our strength as a family as we openly faced this unknown yet inevitable occurrence that stood before us. We called upon the best qualities in each of us to brace our family with the fortitude, courage, and love needed to see us through this chapter. We were all together, hand in hand, solidifying the bonded circle that had always held our hearts and so defined our family.

We reflected on a poignant revelation that certainly put things into perspective. It was a vision of a meadow filled with wildflowers that grew bountifully before our eyes. As we stood among this beautiful foliage, we felt lifted to a brighter sky with brilliant rays of light full of peace and serenity. The symbolism of this vision was prophetic. Despite our life's experiences, challenges, and triumphs in living, all of us sow seeds—people we touch, influence, and cultivate. As time grew nearer to "going home," it was this foliage that served as the ladder—safe passage to an unknown world and life beyond. It was this ladder that, when our day was done, allowed us to travel this journey knowing that a legacy had been left behind and that we *have* lived and made a difference.

As we prepared on this Wednesday, June 25, to enter the waiting room, this revelation provided courage and focus to meet the day's events. With our eyes opened wide and our hearts exposed, we entered the hospital to find Paul's mind wandering with thoughts of days passed and the people who had gone before him, contemplating his future.

As he lay in his hospital bed surrounded by the seeds he had sown and the love he had nurtured through the years, the minutes turned into hours, and time became simultaneously irrelevant and cherished. At midday, Paul's doctor called a family conference to discuss his final life choices; if Paul's mind continued to wander, nature should be allowed to take its course. If otherwise, the choice would be to involve Paul in making the choice—amputate his leg with a fifty-fifty chance of survival, with a questionable recovery followed by a 10–15 percent success rate and continued chemotherapy. What a choice to make! Had we given him every opportunity? As the day progressed, it became apparent that he would choose *his* own.

Paul's room continued to be filled with those who willingly went along with him to places that only *his* mind frequented, countless shouts to loved ones who had passed to lift him and take him "home," only to be interrupted by brief connections to the present and the realities of those he would leave behind.

It was now midnight and the dawn of a new day. The room was quiet; all visitors had left except Donna, Angela, and Noreen (his niece), who stayed to continue this vigil. Barbara, the youngest of the six, left with a heavy heart and great pain. "Could this be the last time?" As the youngest, she had a very defined and close relationship with Paul. At times, many of us felt that he had difficulty translating his perspective of her from the youngest and most in need of his guidance to the wonderful woman and mother she had blossomed into. As she entered her car for the journey home, she exclaimed, "Pop, I am not sure that I can be strong enough to be with you!"

As the morning came near, Paul's heart rate increased, his mind continued to wander, and the multitude of calls to the beyond abounded. He held his hands high and shouted, "Anthony, Janet, Mama—lift me and take me home!" Then, at intervals, he counteracted with loud calls to his wife, Dorothy, sisters Mary and Anna, his children, and grandchildren to bring him back.

Paul's breathing became increasingly labored as his time on earth became diminished. It was now 1:45 a.m. and a do-not-resuscitate order (DNR) was put into place to assure that this imminent journey was uninterrupted by our need to hold on to him. At 2:30 a.m., the head nurse, who intently monitored his condition, joined us in this waiting room. With tears in her eyes, she recalled her father who resided in the Philippines. She had not seen him in five years and was truly taken aback by the demonstrated love that frequented Paul's side. She gently closed the door and asked for permission to embrace him, lovingly reminiscent of the family that she missed so much. She now joined this journey, contributing her learned competence and exposing her awakened heart.

It was now 3:00 a.m. and almost dawn. Donna and Angela left the hospital, realizing that Paul may not return "home" in their presence—his vitals being stable. He was left in the loving care of Cousin Noreen and a compassionate medical team to continue the vigil until his family returned to him. Noreen was always considered a sixth daughter and, as a result, was quite active in Paul's care—administering needles, accompanying him to dialysis, tracking his progress, and the like. Her father, Anthony, (Paul's brother) was sick five years prior, and she devoutly cared for him throughout. After he left this world, she turned to Paul to find solace, guidance, and support. As she continued to hear Paul calling out to her father, she was comforted in knowing that Paul would be safe in his arms, providing him peace during his passage.

We all retreated from the waiting room until that defining moment when, on Thursday, June 26, 2008, at 7:00 a.m., our telephone rang; that dreaded call brought us back to the hospital immediately! It was time to join him as he traveled "home." All of his loving family convened at his side, waiting and watching for his last breath. Mother Christine Petersen Snyder of St. Thomas Church joined us and served as a pillar of faith and support throughout this life-altering experience. In the rush to get back to the hospital, Dorothy had forgotten to take her medicine, upon which she was reliant, necessitating Barbara and her brother-in-law, Michael, to leave for a few moments to get it. Needless to say, they arrived back too late (or not)!

Paul was frightened but never alone, as three generations were gathered to give him strength and courage to greet the light. His mind continued to wander, and his breathing was labored. He was now dependent on an oxygen mask. His eyes opened for a brief moment, trying to utter something to his beautiful wife, Dorothy. In a great statement of valor, she gently whispered to him, "Paul, it's okay to go. You fought hard, and I will be fine. No one can ask more of you!" Then, with his eyes closed and his arms extended, he reached toward his future, into the arms of loved ones who had passed. They welcomed him with open hearts as he called each one of them by name and physically extended himself toward the light he was to behold.

Paul's face became a composite of fear, peace, and joy as he gallantly struggled to hold onto his last breath. He was visibly conflicted between yesterday, today, and the light that now embraced him, desperately trying to hold on to a lifetime of the connections that now surrounded him. Was his work now done? Then, *that* moment arrived. With an inexplicable gesture that transformed his face, his eyes opened wide, and we knew he was welcoming the light as loved ones welcomed him into it.

He was at peace now, no pain, no lifelines, and no regrets! As we processed this wondrous experience, we will always remember the beauty of this defining moment, the dignity and grace in his passing, and we will always cherish his spirit as it now joined others in watching over us, the loved ones he left to carry on!

The Great Celebration

Sarah's Song to Pop

You know that people get rearranged when they are upset
We all miss you; I'll always miss you
In my heart, that's broken now, I have fewer people in my family
You are very important to me
I miss you—everybody misses you
The love is not the same from me
I need you, come back to me, please
Everybody misses you, especially my mother—and me
She was your daughter
I had a weird dream about you tonight—
You were there when I woke up in the morning
My wish came true and I saw you
I was three again in my dream
Then, I told you that you were sick and going to die, and you did…

—Sarah, granddaughter age six

Paul will never know the great lessons that his journey has given to each of us. We will never be the same. As we prepared for this great celebration, we do so with deep sadness and tremendous loss. We were all numb, our hearts were exposed, and there was an incredible void to fill. These lessons now serve as our road map to continue living.

As the networks of people that defined him convened, we were humbled with every act of kindness shown—the flowers, donations to the American Kidney Fund, the food! Everyone made their contribution to this process of defining his life—mourning and healing, each experiencing the outcome of being in this waiting room in their own unique and truly intended way.

The mosaic of people who loved and cared for him stood together now, remembering and reflecting on this life and this legacy…as he faithfully watched!

Processing Loss

Knowing We Are Not Alone

As we continued to process this loss, there were countless Sundays that we sat at graveside, recalling all of the memories and moments that came to pass. Over the year, each "first" underlined the realities in this new chapter in our lives—the first birthday, Christmas, anniversary, Father's Day, and the like. Although physically not present, we felt his spirit in the tranquility of the surrounding open field and gentle wind that seemed to always be present.

It was a December morning with twelve inches of fresh snow on the ground. Determined to keep our Sunday vigil, we diligently arrived at the cemetery. All footstones disappeared in the fallen snow. Armed with only a short-handled brush and an estimate of the gravesite location, we ventured out to experience another life moment captured in the following account, "Angels with a Shovel" by Dorothy Zimmerman.

> Our love of fifty-eight years transcended over two generations of six children and fourteen grandchildren. Our earthly partnership came to a devastating halt when my husband, Paul, passed away after a courageous three-year battle for his life. Although my children and grandchildren have been, and continue to be very supportive of me, I felt a huge void in the activities of daily living.

Sunday morning visits to the cemetery were very comforting to me; as I felt Paul's presence while I sat for hours talking to him at his final resting place. I enjoyed filling him in on family and friend happenings. I didn't feel so alone in making major life-changing decisions after I told Paul all about them. I would always ask my husband for a sign that he heard me. During the three years, he has been gone, I have experienced several incidences that made me feel that Paul has left us only in body, and not in spirit.

Typical of his powerful presence in his earthly life, Paul always sends a blustery wind at the end of our weekly visits. I take this to mean that Paul wants us to realize that he has heard us. I always leave our visits with much-needed confidence for the week ahead, knowing that Paul is watching over our family. It is a given that Paul's blustery wind always starts as we leave the cemetery, regardless of the time of day or season.

Sometimes when we least expect it, the most extraordinary things can happen to ordinary people who believe. It was a freezing Sunday morning after a blizzard that left a knee-deep covering of snow on the ground. Eager to keep our weekly routine, my daughter, my best friend, and I headed to the cemetery after Sunday morning church service. Realizing there wasn't a shovel in the trunk of the car, we decided we could improvise with a small window cleaning brush and our hands. After so many years of weekly visits, we believed the gravesite would be easily found despite the massive amount of snow that had accumulated over it.

As my daughter and I left the car to begin our trek to Paul's grave, we cautioned my best friend to stay in the car as she is disabled and could have gotten hurt in the high snow on the ground. Fighting the inclement weather and using our hands, the brush, and sheer determination, we began clearing what we thought was my husband's gravesite. About a half-hour and four gravesites later, we still had not come across my husband's final resting place.

As the winter weather began to freeze our bodies and our determination, we found what we were looking for. However, clearing the gravesite was almost impossible due to the heavy amount of snow, lack of a shovel, and the diminished use of our hands and feet due to the freezing temperatures. Looking at the virgin snow, we knew we were alone in the cemetery with no one to help us. As my daughter and I realized this was a futile mission, we observed three individuals seeming to be walking toward us in the far distance. As their approach got closer, we noticed the group was comprised of a woman, a man, and a young man who was carrying a shovel. As a chorus of three, they asked if we would like to use their shovel. We gladly accepted the offer and began digging. The woman seemed very happy as we exchanged pleasantries. Her happiness was overtaken by giddiness, which prompted several apologies from her for laughing uncontrollably at a gravesite. The man and the young man spoke not a word and just stood to the side to observe.

As my daughter finished shoveling, she handed the shovel back to the young man. I was bent over using my hands to brush off the little bit of snow that was left on my husband's nameplate. It was then that we both experienced a moment we will never forget. We both looked up to give our heartfelt thanks to these kind strangers. Our words were taken by the blustery winds, that had just started again, and the kind strangers were gone. My daughter and I shared a look of disbelief and looked to the snow for footprints to validate what we just experienced. The snow in the direction from whence the strangers had come, was absent of all footprints. The footprints around Paul's grave belonged only to my daughter and me.

As we trudged back to the car, and my waiting best friend, my daughter and I said not a word to each other as we were trying to come to terms with what had just happened. Bewildered and cold, we were greeted by my best friend asking 'who were those strangers helping you?' as we opened the car door. She wanted to know where they went as they seemed to have just disappeared. Her declaration validated what my daughter and I experienced.

We all agree that on that cold, snow-filled winter day, we were helped with more than just a much-needed shovel. We feel very blessed to have been chosen to experience this extraordinary event. Our belief that our guardian angels are always with us has been strengthened. The understanding that love has no physical or emotional boundaries allows your heart to continue being filled with the guidance of your deceased loved ones.

Reflections from the Waiting Room

Throughout our lives, there are many deliberate experiences to be reflected on with our neighbor, friend, father, and husband, Paul. His most concentrated and sustained gifts, however, were those lessons learned while accompanying him into the *waiting room*. Lessons about life and living, survival, healing, and ultimately, reconciliation were learned there.

Each of us played a role in this journey, and once the blinders were off and our hearts opened, we were transformed.

- First, we understand that everyone has gifts to be shared, and it is through entrusting ourselves into the hearts of others that we truly become connected and fulfilled.
- Secondly, it is never too late to find our way, account for our past, and live our lives with renewed purpose and in concert with these lessons learned.
- Third, even in the darkest moments when the veil is lifted and the blinders off, we are enriched with *every* experience that our hearts come to know.

Further, there are no accidents, and everything around us and every encounter we face, each person, has meaning, perhaps not understood at the moment. Each life matters, and every contribution made is not a blind investment but one with interest collected in the life beyond. Though we can never determine our time, we define ourselves in the moments and life moments leading up to it—and Paul certainly did just that.

Finally, we know that the only thing permanent in this world is change, and our hearts and spirits are transformed in these defining moments. We were taught that there are two options as we enter the waiting room—one, to passively accept the outcomes given; two, to live our lives with renewed and deliberate purpose so that when the dawn is near, we know that we have lived. Death is universal to the human experience. Preparing for it (or not) takes a lifetime.

We are eternally grateful for these lessons we have come to know and his indomitable spirit, courage, and being a true example of love. As a family, we celebrate him this day and forever in our hearts. Not the end, but a renewed beginning. The question remains. What will *you* do the next time *you* enter the waiting room? And *you* will!

Postscript

I know what you are thinking...how many of us remain in the waiting room as we continue to navigate these dynamic COVID-19 times. So much of what we have come to know—how we work, learn, love, celebrate, mourn, communicate, and connect—has been transformed.

As we frequent this place, the *waiting room*, what lessons will *we* come to know? How will *our* lives be transformed? How will *you* live in the waiting room?

About the Authors

Dorothy and Angela Zimmerman are a mother-and-daughter writing team. Dorothy was born in 1934 to German immigrants who settled in the United States. She is a wife, mother of six, grandmother of fourteen, and great-grandmother of eight. Among her greatest contributions is the care and cultivation of her children, their children, and their children's children, and as the main caretaker for her husband of fifty-four years, Paul.

Dorothy received a degree from a local business school and worked as an executive secretary at an insurance firm until she met and married Paul Zimmerman at the early age of eighteen. She spent a lifetime developing her greatest legacy—her family. Then, she returned to the workforce, investing over twenty-two years at a local child care agency. Dorothy is quite extraordinary in that her influence is great as a role model to many, and her perception of herself is humble and reserved.

Angela Zimmerman has an abiding commitment to youth, family, and community development. She served in the health and human services field for over thirty-five years and is a development administrator and instructor in higher education for ten years. Angela holds a master's degree in public and health care administration, is a certified National Family Development Credential and Empowerment Skills for Leaders instructor, and has participated in several certificate programs in personal coaching, leadership, fundraising, and family and community development. She has received numerous local and statewide awards for her work with families and communities. In the words of the author Neil Postman, "children are the living message we send to a time we will not see…" Angela fervently believes that a society's investment in children, families, and communities conveys and projects something about ourselves, our values, and priorities into the future.